TAKING
RESPONSIBILITY
FOR THE CHOICES
WE MAKE.

LEIGHANN McCOY

DaySpring

LIVE YOUR FAITH

First Edition, February 2017

www.dayspring.com

Cover design by Kim Russell | Wahoo Designs

ISBN: 9781684089918

To my daughters, Mikel and Kaleigh,
and my son, TJ.

Mikel, thank you for letting me tell your story
over and over again.

Kaleigh, thank you for writing much
of this book through your text messages.

TJ, thank you for inspiring me to write this book.
It was birthed out of our conversations with one another.

I love you all three more than you can ever imagine!

Mom

TABLE OF CONTENTS

INTRODUCTION

If you picked up this book, you're most likely . . .

- undone
- offended
- wounded
- legitimately angry, or
- somebody's done you wrong.

Or, you've found yourself in an unimaginable place where the goodness of God seems to have left you, and everything you thought you knew about Him and His ways have evaporated in the aftermath of the devastation that brought you here.

I know. I'm with you. I've been undone.

I'm a pastor's wife, and people who seemed to be my friends have wounded me.

I'm also a woman. Plenty of somebodies have done me wrong. They've slandered me, judged my motives harshly, and published their thoughts in subtly sneaky ways on social media.

Don't you hate that?

I'm also a mother. My children have made choices that have hurt me, but more than that, they have experienced things in life that I trusted God to protect them from.

Besides all that, I have fought cancer (twice), lost a brother-in-law and a nephew in tragic accidents, lost my sister to cancer, held a baby when we buried his mother, and held a mother when we buried her baby. Life has happened to me, as I'm sure it's also happened to you. If we sat together on the front porch of my "laughing place" (a ninety-year-old farmhouse in the North Carolina mountains), we could sip sweet tea and share our stories and our tears.

In fact, I have a little plastic pool that my granddaughters love to play in—two, actually. One holds sand (that's pink, of course, because everyone knows that little girls need pink sand to play in) and the other holds rainwater. Not clean, healthy, "Wow! I wish I could taste that water!" That little plastic pool stays filled with the kind of rainwater that gets gunky. If I let it stay there long, I might grow a family of frogs.

While it's not a good place for my granddaughters to play, that little plastic pool filled with gunky rainwater gives me a perfect picture of the pity pool in which I love to play. Too many times, I fill my mental pool with the gunk that comes from replaying failures, offenses, losses, and disappointments. I don't have the sense of a preschooler, and instead of steering clear of that stuff, I get in there, sit down, and splash about. If I can convince friends to join me (which I can do on most occasions), we can sit together with our pumpkin spice lattes (in

the winter) and sweet tea (in the summer) and commis-
erate with one another. Seemingly, the more we splash
about, the deeper the "water" flows.

What about you?

Isn't it incredibly tempting and oh-so natural when
you find yourself . . .

Undone

Offended

Wounded

Legitimately angry

In an unimaginable place where God's goodness
seems to have left you . . . to just jump right in to the
pity pool? From inside that pool, you can blame others
and abdicate all responsibility for the mess you find
yourself in.

This book is about getting out of that pool. If you
like it where you are, this book's not for you.

More specifically, this book is about *how* to get out
of that pool. It's amazing how easy it is to get in and how
hard it seems to get out. You know the way in; assume
that life happens *to* you and forget that life just happens.
I'm proud of you. You are taking the first step out of the
pity pool this very minute by reading this introduction. If
you choose to keep on reading, each chapter will tell you
how to not only get out of your pity pool, but also how to
become empowered to take charge of your life. You have
more power in this journey than you might realize. The
chapter titles themselves give you a step-by-step guide for
accomplishing this great feat.

Within these chapters, I'm going to tell some personal stories (much to the chagrin of my family members and friends), and I'm going to make some personal confessions. But at the end of each chapter, I'm going to stick it to you—and give you an assignment to do. This book might entertain you, it might even inspire you, but it's not going to really help you if you don't complete those assignments. And I'll just go ahead and warn you that there are going to be some days that you don't want to complete those assignments. Do it anyway.

All right! Are we ready? If you want to cry and be a slobbery mess, do it now. Because from this point forward, we're not going to cry anymore. (Well, we might a little, but not too much.) Put your big girl pants on and stop blaming others. Instead, start taking responsibility for the choices you make.

CHAPTER 1:

SHIFT YOUR FOCUS FROM WHAT YOU FEEL TO WHAT IS REAL

If you're like me, you love chocolate. Right now, I'm snacking on dark chocolate M&M's. I poured a handful out on my desktop as an incentive. I told myself that I would eat one piece of candy for every 250 words I wrote.

I just ate five. That should have equaled 1,250 words, but there are only forty-six in that first paragraph. My plan isn't working. But I have been inspired. It just came to me that chocolate and self-pity have several things in common.

1. They both offer a measure of comfort.

Let's just go ahead and admit that we eat chocolate because of the endorphins chocolate releases in our bodies! Seriously, chocolate has been scientifically proven to make you feel better. When I Googled this statement to maintain my integrity as a writer, I discovered that a Cambridge University study actually verified that chocolate does make you feel good; however, not because of a mysterious chemical in it that releases endorphins but simply because it tastes so good.[1] Isn't that great? Something can taste so good that it actually makes you feel good. That might be why I'm now feasting on an apple cake I cooked yesterday that has a cup of vegetable oil and a stick of butter in it. (I am not eating the apple cake with the chocolate. I'm several weeks removed from the first writing of this chapter and decided to just add this tidbit of information because that apple cake is seriously good and it really does make me feel good.)

But back to pity, and this bent we have toward blaming others for the mess we find ourselves in. Pity doesn't necessarily taste good, but it does make you feel good. To sit and soak in the sadness you experience is good to a degree. After all, crying salty tears enables healing to begin! But there's a line between tears that trigger healthy wholeness and those that fill our pools of self-pity. Which brings me to my second comparison of chocolate and pity.

2. They are both bad for you in extreme quantities.

Everyone knows that a piece of "better than sex" chocolate fudge cake is good (I'm not saying it's necessarily

---

1 http://www.dailymail.co.uk/news/article-128858/Scientists-prove-chocolate-better-love.html

able to live up to its name, but it *is* good), but if you eat
the whole cotton-pickin' cake, you're going to be sick.
(You will also get sick if you eat the whole apple cake—
I'm just sayin' that apple cake is almost better than *you
know what*.) In the same way, a sense of self-pity and
expression of it in moderation is actually good. Taking
time to process, ponder, and reflect is good for you. But
if you indulge in too much pondering and reflection,
you're going to get stuck; especially if your processing,
pondering, and reflection consistently lay blame for your
mess at the feet of someone other than yourself. We will
discuss this more throughout this book.

Now is a good time to define the word *pity* (so you'll
not be distracted by the fact that I just used the words
sex and *chocolate* in the same sentence).

Pity: sympathy or sorrow for the suffering of others;
something that causes regret.[2]

So the word *pity* is more often related to a feeling
that you share on behalf of someone else (that's why
finding friends to splash about with you in your pity
pool is such an easy thing to do). And when pity shifts
from a focus on others to a focus on oneself, that's when
it tends to get distorted and out of control. Pity makes
that turn when you sort through your mess and subcon-
sciously decide that you were victimized by someone
else's actions or something else that happened to you.

You start casting blame, and before you know it,
you find yourself losing control of your life. You begin

---

2 http://www.thefreedictionary.com/pity

feeling sorry for yourself. Ironically enough, if you are the kind of person who gets stuck in this place of feeling sorry for yourself, you are most likely also the kind of person who can really feel sincere compassion for the hurts and misfortunes of others. A shifting of your focus from your own troubles to theirs will be a key factor in getting out of your pity pool.

There is one more similarity between chocolate and pity.

3. Both chocolate and self-pity are addictive.

I have now eaten the entire handful of M&M's, and I have this urge to go replenish my desktop with more. And I'm only 771 words further along in this chapter, which should have been only three more M&M's if I'm keeping with my 250-word limit.

You see how addictive chocolate can be? Unfortunately, feeling sorry for yourself can be just as addictive. Once you've turned your attention away from others and directed it toward yourself, it's very easy to keep it there. The more you look for the ways you've been done wrong, the more you'll find them. The more you pile up offenses and bad luck and terrible, no-good, very bad things, the deeper your nasty rainwater, frog-friendly little pool will be. Before you know it, your little pity pool has turned into a deep ocean where the waves swell; lightning strikes in the distance, thunder rumbles, and you're . . .

. . . ready to get out.

SHIFT YOUR FOCUS

The first step to getting out of this mess is to shift your focus from what you feel to what is real.

You may not be one of them, but I know plenty of people who are quite good at building altars of disappointment that become high places where they worship the god of disaster.

I have to confess that I know one of these people quite well. She's writing this book.

Here's how this happens. I have a bad day—week, month, year. For goodness' sakes, I've had a bad six years if I want to be completely honest.

How do I know?

Well, in March 2010, I was diagnosed with colon cancer.

In May of that year, our church, the one my husband pastors, was flooded to the tune of $275,000 of damage.

That was in the beginning of May. At the end of May, my first-born high school graduate (cum laude) daughter chose not to go to college; instead, she moved in with her boyfriend and found out she was pregnant.

That all happened in 2010.

In February 2011, my eighteen-year-old daughter became a mother. In March, she married her boyfriend and he said I'd never have anything to do with his daughter. I don't remember much else about that year except that my second daughter graduated salutatorian from high school, and I did get to see my granddaughter . . . quite a bit.

In June 2012, the cancer that was removed in 2010 recurred in my liver. I had surgery to remove the right lobe of my liver and followed that up with six months of chemotherapy. In August 2012, my son "dry-drowned" in my backyard swimming pool. Fortunately, he was saved by our good friend, Zach. In November 2012, my son-in-law was deployed to Afghanistan and my daughter was suffering from depression related to the abuse in her marriage.

In May 2013, my sister was diagnosed with cancer; stage 4 endometrial cancer. My son graduated from high school and then in July of that year, my son-in-law returned from deployment. In October, my daughter hinted at the abuse escalating in her home. And thus began the cycle of leaving then returning, then leaving and returning.

In January 2014, my concerns for my daughter were validated when her neighbor told me she was afraid that if something didn't change, my daughter might lose her life. In March, my daughter came home, pregnant and hurting. In September of that year, my second granddaughter was born.

Then in March 2015, my sister died after her brief twenty-two-month battle with cancer. In June, my son-in-law lost his job with the army and moved back in with my daughter and their girls. Once again, I heard the words, "You will never see our daughters again!" From June to September, I had no contact with my daughter or my granddaughters. In October, my daughter came home for good. Numb, broken, and divorcing.

In January 2016, we let go eight part-time staff members from our church (primarily for budget reasons), which opened a season of frustration-venting targeted at me and my husband on social media. (A season that lasted well into the spring.) In April, I lost a friend I'd had for nearly twenty years. Not to death but to, according to her, my bad behavior. In May, my other daughter fell in love. In June, my daughter's divorce was final. In July, my other daughter's heart was broken. Also in July, a storm left severe damage to my property at my "laughing place."

In fact, I'm sitting on the front porch, gazing out at the storm-torn trees as I write this book.

You see how easy that is to do? How does my altar compare to yours? Is it bigger? Is yours? If we find the highest spot and pile our offenses, disappointments, and hurts up there, everyone can see them. As we build our monuments to severe displeasure, we can name names and chronicle events. We can always find someone or something, or even God, to blame.

I just spent a good portion of this chapter and several minutes of your time inviting you to join me at my altar of disappointment. Or, I could put it another way. I just spent a good portion of this chapter and your time describing to you the agony of being me with a bent toward the terrible, no-good, very bad side of my life. Most likely, you either have joined me in my pity pool. Or, you compared my terrible circumstances to your own and felt a bit better about the pool you're in; or a bit worse, depending on whether or not your stuff is more heartbreaking than mine.

Either way, doing this doesn't get us out of our misery. It only makes things worse.

Instead of piling up your disappointments and letting them settle into a mess, separate them.

Separate them like this: in March 2010, I was diagnosed with colon cancer. Within three weeks, I was in and out of surgery. My friend (whom I later lost) fed me ice chips at the hospital. My husband suffered severe allergies because he insisted on staying by my side and hundreds of people from our congregation showered me with flowers. Seriously, my hospital room smelled like a florist.

My daughter's high school tennis team paid me a visit; they even circled up and prayed over me while they were there. The attendant who pushed me in a wheelchair to the hospital entrance when I was released sang, "The B-I-B-L-E—that's the book for me!" at the top of his lungs *with* my mother all the way to the elevator, through four hallways and out to the curb.

For the first time in my life, I realized my life was fragile. I numbered my days aright (like the Psalmist encourages us to do) and had immediate clarification of my priorities and goals. I now know what it's like to be out of control of things you thought you were in control of; and I had a face-to-face "come to Jesus" moment when I realized that what I thought I believed,

I truly believed. My faith was tested and now I know that I know I will go to heaven when I die and I don't have to be afraid of whatever might take me there.

There you go.

That was me taking my altar down, one stone at a time.

We don't have room in this book for me to disassemble my entire six years, but if we did, you would be amazed at the many ways God proved Himself faithful to me in each and every one of these unbelievably difficult and disappointing things that have happened in the past six years of my life.

What's more important is that you take the time to tear your altar down one stone at a time. I promised you that I would have an activity for you at the end of each chapter. Here it is.

HOW TO TEAR DOWN YOUR ALTAR OF DISAPPOINTMENT

1. First, identify your altar of disappointment.

You can't take down an altar you can't identify. In the Old Testament, many kings' legacies were tainted by this statement: "He did what was right in the sight of the LORD but not wholeheartedly . . . he didn't remove the high places." The "high places" were altars that were either left over from the Canaanite's idol worship, or built by backslidden Jews to worship the pagan gods. When I first recognized this indictment on the kings, I was stung to the core. I realized that in my own life, it could be said, "She did what was right in the sight of the LORD, but not wholeheartedly . . . she didn't remove the high places." That was when I began to study the nature of the high places and discovered that I'd built one of my own.

I hear women describe their altars to me. They begin (like I did) several weeks, months, or years ago when bad stuff started to happen and they start listing all the things that went wrong along with the people who did them wrong. Or, they've experienced something so devastating that they've allowed that one thing to become an altar all by itself and they tell me all the various reasons that one thing has completely derailed their lives.

Right now, take time to make a list on paper (like I did) of the various disappointments, offenses, and tragedies that have piled up in your head and heart. If you are someone who has experienced one devastation, make your list of all the reasons this one thing has caused you so much pain. This will not be hard to do.

2. **Take that list in your hands and pray this prayer:**

> *Lord, I confess that this isn't merely a historical account of my life; it's a pile of hurt that I've allowed to become an altar of disappointment. I'm disappointed in myself, in (you fill in the blank here), and if I'm honest, I'm disappointed in You. Even so, I don't want to be this person who "worships"*

at this altar. Forgive me for building this altar that casts shadows on my faith and clouds my ability to see Your face. I want to tear this altar down. For You, for me, for Jesus's sake. Please help me take this altar apart. In Jesus's name I pray. Amen.

3. **Now, take each item on your list one at a time, and answer these questions regarding that one thing:**

   • How did God reveal Himself to you on that day (when that happened, at that time)?
   • Who came alongside you to ease your pain?
   • What insight or understanding did you gain from that experience?
   • Now that you have that insight and understanding, what are you able to do that you could not do before?

4. **Don't leave one stone on that altar of disappointment.**

If we had real stones and were building real altars, we could give each stone a name. For instance, my "cancer" stone could be renamed "confident of my heavenly home." Actually, that one stone would become several: "outpouring of love," "relief from busyness and confusion," "able to comfort others"—the stones I could carve from that one rock are many!

If we took the time to rename each stone, we could build an altar much greater that would honor God and encourage us!

Take the time to evaluate how you feel, remember the faithfulness of God in the midst of your suffering, and choose to shift your focus from how you feel to what is real. This will take some time, but it will be time well spent.

CHAPTER 2:

KNOW WHAT IS REAL

"The real problem is not why some pious, humble, believing people suffer, but why some do not."

—C. S. LEWIS

I find this a refreshing quote after that laborious task of disassembling my altar of disappointment. I promised you some personal confessions. Here's one: when I was diagnosed with cancer, Tom and I were traveling toward the interstate to go into town (Nashville) for me to have a PET scan. I was still reeling from the fact that I—*I*—had cancer. It wasn't fair. I was faithful to exercise, I tried to eat right, I refused to give my children sugary cereals or Twinkies. That should've counted for something! We came to a traffic light and a car full of smokers pulled up beside us. Did I mention that I'm not a smoker? I've never taken a puff on anything more than a bubble gum cigarette when I was a kid. I looked at those people smoking their cigarettes and said, "Why do I have cancer and not them?"

Ugh! I cringe to think that those words came out of

my mouth. I am sobered to recognize the critical, judgmental spirit they expose. But seriously, I was dealing with what C. S. Lewis mentioned: "The real problem is not why some pious, humble, believing people suffer, but (let me divert from Mr. Lewis here) why some who aren't pious, humble, and believing don't."

As I think of all the people who might read this book, I can't help but wonder what kind of stuff you're dealing with. I am fairly certain that if we were to share that glass of iced tea on my porch, I would invite you to share your story and then I would say things like:

"No! I can't believe that!"

"You poor soul."

"I am so very sorry."

"That's terrible."

And other statements that might "bless your heart" but wouldn't do a single thing to get you out of your pity pool. This chapter is about dealing with reality. And by dealing, I mean *accepting*.

I enjoy playing cards. Rook and Spades are two of my all-time favorite card games. In any card game, the dealer deals the cards, and you play with the hand you're dealt. It doesn't matter if you don't like your hand, and it doesn't matter if you don't have a good hand. It doesn't matter if you're like my father-in-law who, on more than one occasion, muttered, "I would spit if I thought it would do any good." You don't get to choose which cards come to you. You know what's out there, and you know everyone at the table is going to get something. You hope you get the better things, but you have to be satisfied with what you get. You have to also be savvy if you're dealt the worst hand at the table.

In the game of life, I have to agree with C. S. Lewis. But I'm not quite as other-centered in my honest estimation. My real thought is, "Why did I have to go through these things and not them?" Until I was the one going through "stuff," I felt real sorry for the others. But then when I became the "others," I found myself comparing my stuff to theirs and that never ends well. So instead of playing a game of comparison and instead of spitting (which does no good at all), let's take a minute or two to state the facts. For I believe that if you see the truth on paper, you will better be able to accept the truth in your heart. And to know the truth is to be set free from living your life at the expense and mercy of others. Living your life at the expense and mercy of others is exactly what you do when you play the blame game.

WHAT IS REAL ABOUT LIFE?

One of the most powerful lessons I've learned is that my perception of life will either set me up for incredible surprise (in a good way) or incredible disillusion (in a bad way). I learned this lesson best as a young pastor's wife. The funny thing about growing up in a big church and then marrying a young seminary student is that you might find yourself in a small church for the very first time in your life. And small churches operate much differently than large churches operate. Not only that, but the life of a pastor's wife looks way different from the outside than it does from the inside.

When I was a teenager, I thought my pastor's wife was the coolest person ever. She was gracious, real, funny, kind; and she seemed to have a great marriage and the cutest kids. Everyone knew her and everyone loved her, or so I thought. I couldn't imagine a better life than to be a pastor's wife. Just think of the fun of being known by all the church members, being loved by them, and filling your hours with service to the Lord in my most favorite place on earth, His church.

It wasn't too many months into the role of pastor's wife that I discovered that everyone knowing you wasn't all it was cracked up to be. When people know you, they critique you. If you wear your sweats to the grocery store, they notice. A few months after I realized that my sweats weren't appropriate grocery attire, I found out that not all our congregants liked me. They got to have opinions about the way I served the church and whether or not I smiled and greeted them when I walked past them. Then, the worst of all happened: I discovered that they didn't all adore my husband as much as I did. It was a rude awakening. My reality check was not the hard part; it was the preconceived notion that life as a pastor's wife was going to be wonderful. Thinking one thing and realizing another is what made it so hard.

We are like that. We develop preconceived notions

about what life is *supposed to be*, and then we get all discombobulated when it doesn't turn out to be what we think it ought to be. My remedy for this is to tell you five things that are real about life. If you will accept these realities, you will discover that it's easier than you might have thought to take your life by the horns and direct it in a way that frees you from your pity pool and empowers you to live above the fray.

Here are five realities of life:

1. Failure is real.

My son is an entrepreneur. And like many entrepreneurs, he reads voraciously. Fortunate for me, he shares his findings. One of the first things TJ taught me was that most successful people consider failure a stepping-stone to the realization of their dreams. They embrace failure by seeking to find the lesson hidden in it. TJ explained that unsuccessful people see failure as something to be avoided at all costs. But successful people understand that failure is a part of life. Therefore, they don't run from failure when it comes their way. Instead, they seek to invest the lesson they learn in the experience into their ongoing journey toward success.

Here's a story to illustrate. Henry Ford transformed the automobile industry with assembly line production and his Model T. But did you know that before Ford succeeded with the Ford Motor Company, he failed not once but twice? Both of Ford's business failures resulted in bankruptcy. Henry Ford was twice the failure, but that didn't matter because he was once a success and Ford's success changed the world.

To accept failure as a very real part of life changes how I look at things when I experience failure.

I've failed plenty of times. I've failed at friendship, and I've failed at work. I've failed at cooking (on multiple occasions), and I failed as a parent and a wife and a speaker and, goodness, I can't think of any area of my life where I haven't failed! But rather than see those failures as hard lessons learned, I fell prey to the Devil's lies and allowed my failures to discourage me from trying again. I also allowed those failures to heap shame on me.

Shame that tore away at my confidence.

Shame that turned me inward.

Shame that made the water in my pity pool feel just about right so that I stayed there a bit longer.

Failure is a reality. I've failed. You've failed. Everyone on the face of the earth has failed (except Jesus— He never fails!). Learn to accept failure as a valuable lesson and learn from your mistakes.

2. Disappointment is real.

You knew this already, didn't you?

Life gets really real when you're dealt a disappointing hand. I had a harsh conversation once with another person. (Which also goes down on record as one of those failure times in my life.) She was comparing her life to mine. She was single, I was married. She didn't have much money, I had a little more. She was living a life she never dreamt of living, I was, from her point of view, living my dream. She was feeling a whole lot like I felt that day I looked at the car full of smokers and wished . . . well, you know what I wished.

She was splashing about in her pity pool, and I was preaching. (I don't recommend doing this. I told you this is one of my failures in relationship experiences.) This is what I eloquently said: "I am sorry you've been dealt the cards you're holding in your hand. I am sorry that you think the cards in my hand are much better than yours. But you don't get to play my cards, and I don't get to play yours. Stop whining over what you don't have in your hand, and stop wishing you had what was in mine. Stop assuming you know what it's like to sit in my seat at the table, and play the cards you've been dealt!"

I know, you're glad you aren't my friend, right?

I share that humiliating glimpse into my personal life to say, disappointment is a part of life. Some people are going to seem to live lives that are pretty near perfect. Some of those who seem to have perfect lives really do have great lives. Sometimes those practically perfect people are going to be obnoxious about it (especially now that they can post pictures of their great life on social media). And they will be the people who are most ready to share advice with you when you feel a little defeated. After all, they are on top of the world, and you are struggling to climb up there.

Some people are going to have it not so great. They

won't deserve "not so great," but those who have it great might think that they do. They can't help it. Their life experiences cause them to make assumptions about others. In their unintentional processing of their success, they assume that they got themselves up there by making the right choices and opening the right doors. They don't know that you can make the right choices and not get the right results. They also don't know what it's like to turn the doorknobs and find most doors locked. They might make up all kinds of reasons why they have it good and their friends don't. They might be wrong, and their petty remarks on Facebook will tick you off, but don't be snarky back, especially not there—that won't help you feel any better.

Some people won't ever know what it's like to feel your particular pain. And so they don't know how feeling that pain impacts the decisions you make. Others will feel your pain, they will understand. Some people will never have it as bad as you, others will never have it as good.

Disappointment is a very real fact of life. People who choose to accept this reality become stronger. They take their hard knocks in life, brush off the bruising, and get back out there. My daughter gave her dad and me a great illustration of how one does this one afternoon in our backyard. I wrote an article about it in a magazine. I've got a copy of it hanging in my house. It's titled, "Just Keep Swinging." I'll borrow an excerpt from it here.

When Mikel was in middle school, she wanted to try out for the softball team. She'd played slow pitch softball for years but discovered on the first day of try-outs that the middle school team was playing fast pitch softball. Her dad wasn't about to let her be intimidated by this "minor" detail, so he assured her that he would work with her and teach her how to hit a fast pitch. After practice at school, Tom and Mikel took their bucket of balls to the backyard. Mikel stepped up to the glove that marked home plate. Tom threw the ball as fast as he could, underhanded. Although his aim was good, his speed was off, so he decided to try an overhanded throw and hum the softball like a baseball.

"You ready, Mikel?" her dad called out.

"Um hmmm." Mikel pulled her bat back and took her position. Tom took aim, pitched the softball as fast as he could, and . . .

Hit Mikel right upside her head.

The ball knocked her to the ground. Mikel cried, and her sister Kaleigh (who was playing in the field) ran to her and cried, and Tom cried. Everyone was a blubbering mess; I was watching all this from the kitchen window.

"I'm sorry! I didn't mean to!" Dad cried.

"How could you do that?" Kaleigh cried.

"It's okay, Daddy," Mikel cried.

After everyone was finished crying, Kaleigh and Tom watched as Mikel got to her feet and walked out of the backyard and into the garage. A few minutes later, she came out of the garage with her bicycle helmet on her head. She stepped up to the plate, pulled her bat back, and said, "I'm ready, Daddy, throw it again!"[3]

Life will disappoint you. Sometimes, it will knock you down. When it does, go get your helmet, put it on your head, pull your bat back, and yell at the top of your lungs, "I'm ready! Throw it again!"

3. Crisis is real.

Sudden disaster, unexpected loss, and terrible interruptions happen. They happen in the daytime and they happen at night. I cringe every time my phone rings after midnight. The most recent time this happened, the phone rang just before 3:00 a.m. I answered it and learned that a friend's eighteen-year-old son left his girlfriend's house late that night. His car apparently ran off the road and into a ditch and he died. Just like that, a mother lost her son; a sister lost her brother; a father lost his boy; and a girlfriend lost the boy she loved.

A curve, a wet road, a bald tire, a squirrel running across the street, a sleepy boy . . . gone.

Crisis is real. And the real nature of crisis is that it can happen to anyone at any time.

My friend's daughter got sick with the flu. Her family's spring break plans were spoiled. And then . . . she died.

My nephew was just making a quick run to the gas station in the middle of the night, when he and his friends spun out of control, hit a tree, and their truck

---

3 Leighann McCoy, "Just Keep Swinging," *Leading Adults*, Spring 2005.

burst into flames. In a moment, my brother-in-law lost his only son. That same brother-in-law lost his wife to a rare lung disease just a year or so before his son was killed in that wreck. The young girls wailed at that funeral. I can still hear them now.

Crisis is real. It comes in all different ways. Terrorists fly commercial planes into the World Trade Center, tornadoes rip across the plains, tidal waves wipe out entire coastal regions, hurricanes create such force that levies give way, cyclists are hit by cars, and tiny little babies lose their battles to live. You may be in your pity pool because crisis is real. I'm not even going to try to compare the loss of my trees to the loss of your child, or parent, or spouse, or house, or income, or limbs, or . . .

Crisis is real. It is a very real, very hard part of life. When we understand that we are in no way guaranteed a life without crises, we learn to appreciate the days we have when we are crisis-free. To accept the reality that crises can happen to anyone at any time, is not to live under the oppression of impending doom but rather to humbly accept crisis when it comes your way and choose to trust God through it.

One person said, "Conflict builds character. Crisis defines it."

4. Shattered dreams are real.

I have a beautiful friend. She's like Martha Stewart at home and Anne Sullivan in the classroom (Anne Sullivan was the incredible teacher whose patience broke through to Helen Keller in her dark world). Her children grew up, they went to college after high school, one of them is married, and he and his wife are expecting their first child. My friend and her husband got to rejoice at their son's wedding. I attended their son's wedding, and it was beautiful. My daughter Kaleigh and I voted it the most gorgeous wedding of that summer's wedding season. My friend and her husband got to smile and pray and celebrate God's goodness in delivering the daughter-in-law they'd been praying for ever since they learned they were having a baby boy.

I haven't gotten to do that. My daughter didn't have a wedding. She got married at the office of the Justice of Peace. I went to bed on Friday night, then woke up the next morning and saw that her status and her name had changed on Facebook.

I'm not like Martha Stewart at home either. My home looks more like a disheveled shelter for vagabonds than it does a peaceful place to rest. If we have home-cooked meals, it's because someone's been invited to dinner.

I prayed for my children's spouses too! Things just didn't turn out the way I thought they would. A few years ago, a dear friend invited me to speak at her event in Nashville. We were at the Opryland Hotel and Gloria Gaither was on the program. The theme for the weekend was "Something Beautiful," which, of course, led me to think of the song the Gaithers wrote by that same name.

I titled my message, "Something Beautiful, Something Good," and I quoted a few lines of the song. If you're humming the music now, then you may already be aware of the incredible message written in the first verse:

> *If there ever were dreams*
> *That were lofty and noble*
> *They were my dreams at the start*
> *And hope for life's best were the hopes*
> *That I harbor down deep in my heart*
> *But my dreams turned to ashes*
> *And my castles all crumbled, my fortune*
> *turned to loss*
> *So I wrapped it all in the rags of life*
> *And laid it at the cross*[4]

Pretty powerful, huh? Even Bill and Gloria Gaither must have had personal experience with shattered dreams. I haven't asked her, but I would imagine that my Martha Stewart/Anne Sullivan friend has probably experienced her fair share of shattered dreams as well, even if I'm not seeing them.

Shattered dreams are real, and they happen to everyone. You may not know it, but most people around you are dealing with the aftereffects of dreams shattered. Don't be duped into thinking that only you have suffered the loss of your dreams.

When my children were little, I wanted so much for them to dream big dreams and live to see them fulfilled. I thought that if their dreams ever shattered, they would

---

4 http://www.lyricsmode.com/lyrics/b/bill_gaither/something_beautiful.html

shatter too. I'm living on the other side of some pretty big dreams shattered to smithereens and I'm here to tell you, those dreams might shatter—some definitely will. But you don't shatter with them and the great thing about dreams is that new dreams can replace the old ones.

5. Life is real . . .

Hard.
That's it, my friends.
Life is real hard.

LET'S GET REAL

I know this chapter hasn't been much fun. And most likely, I didn't tell you anything you didn't already know. But it's time nonetheless to do your homework.

1. Make a list of the five things I've told you are real.
2. Did I forget anything? Add those realities to your list.
3. Consider which of these realities you've argued with the most. Circle that one.
4. Pray this prayer:

   Father, I know these things are real. That doesn't make them easier to experience. I've (failed/been disappointed/experienced this crisis/had my dreams shattered) and my life is hard right now—real hard. I'm confused, I'm hurt, and I need You. I need to know that You are with me and that together we can make it. Father, I could place my trust in human psychology, worldly success, even other religions, but I choose this minute to lean into You. I choose to trust that You are going to show me the way out of this mess and into Your presence where Your peace swallows my pain. In Jesus's name I pray. Amen.

CHAPTER 3:

KNOW WHAT IS REAL ABOUT YOUR RELATIONSHIP WITH GOD

You're going to like this chapter much better than the last one. While life really is full of failure and disappointment—and even though crises can hit at any moment; although your dreams may shatter and your journey through life might be especially hard—God is real. And our very real God has made a way for us to have a very real relationship with Him.

The important thing is to understand what is real (as opposed to what is not real) about this relationship we get to have with God. I'm going to discuss three things that are real about your relationship with God and then tell you four things you're *really* going to like related to those three things.

1. You've really been saved from your sin to live forever.

This is the good news.

When you invited Jesus to rule and to reign in your life—when you accepted His extravagant gift of salvation and experienced the forgiveness of your sins—you were really saved from your sin to live with God in a personal relationship forever.

The night Jesus was born, God sent angels to shepherds so we'd know that Jesus came for everyone; not just the ones who were sleeping in beds that night in Bethlehem. God sent a star to wise men in the East so we'd know that Jesus came for those who were near and those who were far away; those who were rich and those who were poor.

This is the good news.

This is good news that delivers great joy.

We forget that sometimes. We forget the joy of our salvation.

In our pools of pity, we wonder why the God of the Universe, who came to save our souls, isn't saving us from *this* or from *that*. We focus on what God is not doing and neglect to ponder the incredible work He has already done. We forget that He gave us exactly what we needed when He gave us His Son. In our whining and complaining, we forget that our most desperate need was for a Savior; One who could save us from our sins and ourselves and this sin-stained world.

We forget that when Jesus cried out, "It is finished!" He paid the full price for our sins. We forget that when our Savior hung on the cross, He went there willingly to step in and be a substitute sacrifice so that He, and not we, would pay the wages of sin, which is death. We forget that God knows all things and does all things well.

When we forget these things, we lose the inexpressible joy of the resurrection and the mystery of the power that is ours when we have a personal, dynamic, real relationship with God. We fail to exercise the power of our privileged position in Christ because the Devil has distracted us from serious consideration of the holiness of God, and he's convinced us that there are earthly excuses for the sin that so easily entangles us and estranges us from God.

Did you catch that? I went straight from talking about living with power to talking about sin; and not just any sin, but rather your sin and mine.

If you have received God's precious gift of salvation, you have already accepted the reality of your sin. You've recognized the seriousness of sin's offense against a holy God. If you are confused about the seriousness of sin, just ponder the cross. Many people get all bumfuzzled by the brutality of Jesus's crucifixion. Let me unpack that for just a moment.

Jesus was crucified as a sacrifice for our sins—a sacrifice that was absolutely necessary to appease (or be acceptable to) the holiness of God without compromising God's holiness one iota. The God of the Universe who knew, before He ever created mankind, that sin would destroy His creation; *that* God considered the price He would pay to release the souls of men from their own sin, and chose to create man (and woman) anyway.

So, in the fullness of time, the God of the Universe sent His *very own* Son to be born of a virgin. Jesus was born to Mary, He lived a sinless life, and willingly gave Himself over to be crucified for our sins.

Crucified.

A torturous death penalty that was in place *at that time*. The time that God determined was the right time.

The God of the Universe is holy.

His nature is holy.

Holiness, by nature, is *without sin*.

Apart from Jesus's gift of salvation, we cannot be close to God. Our sin has to stay away from God. The nature of God cannot be tainted by the nature of man. He would not be the Holy God if He allowed the sin of man to contaminate Him.

But the love of God found us irresistible.

Think about that.

God finds you irresistible.

So He sent His Son, His God-man boy to be one of us. Jesus was like us and like God. He was the Son of God and the Son of man. Jesus was divine and human. He was human without sin. Jesus was holy.

Jesus's death was preordained; it was orchestrated, predetermined, prophesied, and expected. Even Jesus knew it was coming. His sinless life was the perfect sacrifice, the only one that would satisfy the holiness of God. Jesus became sin. He took your place and mine and allowed the wrath of God to be poured out on sin.

Sin that Jesus never committed, sin that we could never escape.

On the cross, the Lion (righteous and holy God of the Universe) laid down with the Lamb (the Son of God who so loved the world). (See Isaiah 11.) He did this for you. He did this for me.

And when Jesus died, his death opened heaven's gates and allowed you to enter in.

Jesus was the door.

He was the gate.

He is the way.

Jesus is the only way to have a personal, dynamic, real relationship with God.

When Jesus rose from the dead, He proved to all mankind that His perfect sacrifice satisfied God's perfect holiness and broke the chains of death. These were chains the Devil held until Jesus overcame.

This is good news. Today, you can live your life out from under the shadow of death. Yes, you will die someday. But no! Death will not be the end of you! Knowing that you have an eternal home in heaven united with God untainted by sin ought to be reason enough to think about getting out of your pity pool and taking a look around and releasing anyone or anything from having control over you.

2. **You've really been warned that life on earth will continue to be real—hard; maybe even harder because you've chosen to follow Jesus.**

I love that in the Bible God tells us the truth. I'm amazed at how often we completely miss it. Jesus warned His disciples that if they chose to follow Him, they would encounter many difficulties along the way. He seemed to reassure them that no matter how bad things got, that in the end, when they got to heaven to live with Him, His reward would be so overwhelming that they would consider all other things lost in comparison.

If I were reading this book, I'd stop right here and say, "Okay, show me!"

How about this?

- The parable about the man and the pearl of great price that he found in a field. Read that story in Matthew 13.

Jesus also flat out told His followers that they were choosing trouble when they chose to follow Him:

- The world will hate you (Mark 13:13).
- And He assured them that "in this world" they would have "trouble."
- In this world, you will have trouble, but take heart (John 16:33)!

Many of us misunderstood our salvation. We thought that Jesus came to save us from our troubles when He really came to save us from our sins. Our troubles don't come from the Lord, but neither does the Lord rescue us from all of them. Often God allows our troubles to come into our lives in order to serve God's greater purpose of molding us into the image of Christ. Consider Paul's words in II Corinthians 3:18:

> *"And we all, who with unveiled faces contemplate the Lord's glory, **are being transformed into his image** with ever-increasing glory, which comes from the Lord, who is the Spirit."*

Choosing Christ will get you to heaven when you die, but it won't get you a get-out-of-trouble free card when you are alive on earth. In fact, the decision you made to follow Christ came with a price tag. Jesus said, that in order to follow Him, you must "deny yourself" and "take up your cross daily." Be sure to understand that trouble is guaranteed in this life.

And this brings me to the third reality regarding your relationship with God.

3. **You've really been invited to walk a narrow road—a road less traveled; one where the air gets thick; where the way is hard; and where what matters most is anchored in a place you'll never find on earth.**

This narrow road in life is the part we forget. Jesus told the people who were curious about Him,

"Enter through the narrow gate. For wide is the

gate and broad is the road that leads to destruction, and many enter through it. But small is the gate and narrow the road that leads to life, and only a few find it" (Matthew 7:13–14 NIV).

A few days ago, I took a hike (literally) with my husband and a few friends. It was a gorgeous path across a grassy ridge at the top of Roane Mountain State Park in east Tennessee. As we hiked along the grassy ridge, the trail followed a rocky path. Before I knew it, the rocks were closing in on me, and the breeze that had been making our sunny summer day bearable was choked out by the narrow way. When I think of Jesus's description of what we can expect life to be like when we follow Him, I think of the stifling heat I encountered on that trail.

A few years ago, I was visiting a remote village in India. We drove into the village on what looked like a path. At one point, our car squeezed between two rock walls. The path was so tight that I almost lost my breath. I had to concentrate in order to resist a foreboding sense of claustrophobia. The way was so narrow that had our car stalled, the roof would've had to be lifted off to get us out.

Most people on earth live their lives traveling the broad path. Life on the broad path is centered on self. To follow Jesus is to re-center your life around Him. To follow Jesus is to lose your life; to resist the shortcuts that pop up here and there and to sink your investment of time, emotional energy, and talent into a life that exists beyond the grave in an eternity that you accept by faith.

When you choose the narrow road, you choose to let God keep score. You choose to trust Him when you are disappointed and your dreams are shattered. Like Much Afraid in Hannah Hurnard's *Hinds' Feet on High Places,* you let your Good Shepherd partner you up with the most peculiar traveling companions, Sorrow and Suffering. And along the way, you rest in what you don't know and sacrifice the deepest desires of your heart amidst angst and confusion on the altar of total and complete surrender. You cling tenaciously to the promises in God's Word and beg Him to speak to you out of the dark places.

When you leave the broad path and take the narrow road, you trust Him when all hell seemingly breaks loose against you, because you are confident that He who began a good work in you will carry it through to completion (Philippians 1:6).

Have you heard of the classic work I just referenced, *Hinds' Feet on High Places?* It's a great allegorical tale of a young girl named Much Afraid who dares to take the narrow road. If you like allegories, you will love the story of Much Afraid's journey to the high places. Her story reminds you that those things that have caused you to land in the place you find yourself today did not catch God off guard.

Much to your chagrin, at some point, you have to come to a place where you wrestle hard with the realization that the God of the Universe who saved your soul actually allowed this terribleness to happen to you. And since He did, you can be sure that He will use it to do a work in you that would otherwise never happen. You can also be sure that whatever God is doing in you is in preparation for what God wants to do through you.

Not many people choose the narrow path.

Will you?

There you have it, three realities related to your relationship with God:

1. You've really been saved from your sin to live with God forever.
2. You've really been warned that life on earth will continue to be real—hard; maybe even harder because you've chosen to follow Jesus.
3. You've really been invited to walk a narrow road—a road less traveled; one where the air gets thick; where the way is hard; and where what matters most is anchored in a place you'll never find on earth.

FOUR THINGS YOU CAN EXPECT FROM YOUR RELATIONSHIP WITH GOD:

And here's the part I promised you: four things you can expect from your relationship with God:

1. You can expect to never be alone.

God promises to be present in your trouble and in your good times too. God promises to be with you. The *withness* of God is one of the richest, most rewarding aspects of being in a relationship with Him. The Psalmist spoke of this in Psalm 139. No matter where you find yourself, God is there.

I was in my bathtub one night. My daughter's baby was overdue. My not-yet son-in-law still refused to have anything to do with me and my husband. And even though I had a fragile relationship with my daughter, I didn't have any hope that she would choose me above her main man once we got to the hospital for her to have her baby. I ached over the thought of what it would be like to be separated from my teenaged daughter while she gave birth to her baby.

While taking my bath, I was thinking these thoughts and to be quite honest with you, I was put out with God. I'd prayed, read my Bible, worshiped, fasted, stepped out in faith—and still, my daughter was not where I wanted her to be; and my situation was not the way I wanted it to be; and I was not able to imagine how I was going to survive the upcoming ordeal at the hospital.

I told God He'd failed me.

I told Him He was asking too much of me.

I told Him I was done with this nonsense and ready to return to the relationship He and I had before my life was turned upside down and inside out.

And God actually responded to me. I didn't hear Him with my ears, but rather with my heart. He said,

"Okay, Leighann. So this is it then? We quit? You want me to leave you now?"

I didn't expect Him to say that. I expected Him to reassure me that even though these days had been hard, He was going to see me through and that very soon my heart's ache and longing was going to be satisfied. I didn't expect Him to be so agreeable to leaving me alone.

For a moment, I was silent. I tried to imagine what my life would be like if God left me. And a desperate loneliness threatened to overtake me in that brief second of imagining my life apart from God. Very quickly, I acquiesced. I rescinded my tirade and quietly confessed, "Lord, I don't know how I would get out of this bathtub without You."

I wish I could tell you that God made everything right after that moment. But the experience at the hospital was worse than I imagined it would be. My daughter took four long days to have that baby and she didn't have much to do with me during that time. Looking back, I guess she really did have a worse time than me, but at the time, I was not certain that was what was happening.

I had friends who came to keep vigil with me, but their vigil unsettled me when I faced the pity they had for us in their eyes. One friend was a gem, but the others hovered and their presence accentuated my shame and grief. Those were the worst of times. Tom and I suffered through them together and both decided they were the part of our wedding vows that were included when we said, "For better or for worse . . ."

But, even as I reflect on that nightmare while writing this today, I remember that I was never alone. God was with me in that waiting room. He was with me in the hospital dining room where my friends ate cornflakes and didn't know what to say. God was with me when I tackled the little Indian doctor and begged her to tell me something, anything, about what was happening with my daughter. (Bless her heart, she told me a C-section was coming in the near future, which was God's mercy on me, because she really wasn't supposed to tell me anything.) God seemed like He was sleeping in my storm, but He was *with me* in my boat.

No matter where you find yourself, God is there.

2. You can expect to be taken seriously when you pray.

God promises to listen when you pray. Not only does God promise to hear your prayers, but He also assures you that He will answer your prayers. He encourages you to come boldly into His throne room and tell Him what's on your mind (Hebrews 4:16).

I've spent my entire adult life exploring the mystery of prayer. I've written sixteen books and countless blog posts, taught hundreds of conferences, and most recently created numerous online courses and still this marvelous invitation to pray baffles me. To think that the Creator and Sustainer of the Universe invites you and me into a relationship where He longs for us to

share with Him what's on our hearts and in our minds.
More amazing than that God invites us to pray is this truth: the Creator and Sustainer of the Universe desires to have such intimate communion with us, and He longs to share what is on His heart and mind *so much so,* that He often lingers in releasing His power and waits to accomplish His plans until He knows that we know what He's up to, and we share His passion for His purposes to be accomplished. God longs to partner with us through prayer.

God takes prayer seriously. You can expect to be taken seriously when you pray.

3. You can expect to become more and more like Christ.

If you are not becoming more like Christ, then you might need to take notice of whether or not you are serious about your commitment to follow Him. In Jesus's day, disciples willingly submitted themselves to the authority and teaching of the rabbi they chose to follow. I found an interesting article written on this subject. Check out this summary statement by Doug Greenwold about first-century disciples:

> "The essential qualities of first-century disciples were desire and submission and assumed that emulation, biblical literacy, community, transparency and a willingness to wrestle with God's word were a 'given.' This included a

passion together with zeal to give up any and all of their preconceived notions of how to live one's life and then to embrace the behavior that their rabbi deemed best to honor God. It was a radical, willing, and **totally conforming submission** to the interpretive authority of their rabbi."[5]

What a powerful understanding of discipleship. Jesus's disciples lived in community with Him sincerely studying His way of life. They feasted on the words that came out of His mouth and wrestled with Scripture. Jesus's disciples followed Jesus, understanding full well that their lives would be different today than they would be tomorrow. They expected to change and to grow and to become.

When Jesus charged His disciples to go and make other disciples, they received their commission as a command to go and seek others who were willing and eager to experience the same growth and change that they were experiencing. I'm not sure that we fully embrace that growth and change are essential aspects of our personal, dynamic relationship with God.

I want you to read a text message I received from my daughter Kaleigh a few days ago (this is the daughter whose heart was broken):

●●●●○ AT&T 4G 8:11 AM ⎍ ☀ 100%■

< Messages **Kaleigh** Details

Christlike of you to reach out to her. ♥ yes Mammer and Poppop are coming and 9065

Text Message
Sat, Jul 23, 5:05 PM

The answer to the question "Why did God let this happen?" is always the same. "To make you more like me." God is not in the business of making us comfortable and he's not in the business of making us happy. He's in the business of making us holy.

That'll preach

[○] iMessage ●

---

5 Doug Greenwold, https://bible.org/article/being-first-century-disciple.

Kaleigh is spot on. God isn't working to make us happy. He's working to make us holy. Because God knows that deep down inside you, there is a soul that is happy only when it is holy. When you are walking with Christ, you can expect to become more and more like Christ.

4. You can expect to overcome no matter what comes your way.

Now if that doesn't excite you, I don't know what will. You are an overcomer! There is nothing this world, or the Devil, can toss your way that you, with the companionship power of Christ, cannot overcome.

Don't mistake overcoming for feeling better or getting your own way or not having to suffer along the way. But do know that when all is said and done, whatever it is that has been said and done to you will be woven together for your good and God's glory.

We will talk much more about the wonder of this truth throughout the rest of this book.

REFLECT ON THE REALITY OF YOUR RELATIONSHIP WITH GOD

I hope that your relationship with God is *real*. Consider your honest response to these questions:

• How have I sensed God's presence in my life this year? This month? This week? Today?

- When I read the Bible, does it seem to speak specifically to me?
- When I hear a sermon, does it seem like the preacher knows me?
- When I hear worship music, do I want to sing? Dance? Bow down? Cry? Laugh? Close my eyes?
- When I cheat, lie, or steal, am I more afraid of getting caught or am I sincerely sorry for what I have done?

Your honest response to these questions will help you determine if your relationship with God is real. If your relationship with God is formal, you will miss out on experiencing the reality of the four amazing benefits that are yours when you have a personal relationship with God. Make these four benefits your own by professing them aloud. If you are alone, shout these truths loudly. It will be fun—I promise!

1. Because I am His and He is mine, I AM NEVER ALONE!
2. Because God knows my name, I CAN EXPECT HIM TO HEAR ME WHEN I PRAY!
3. Because we are in a growing relationship with one another, I WILL BE MORE LIKE CHRIST TOMORROW THAN I AM TODAY!
4. Because I have a personal relationship with the Lord of the Universe, I WILL OVERCOME!

CHAPTER 4:

GET UP!

In these first few chapters, we've talked about realities. The reality is that you are in this place today because you've been confronted with most likely one or more of the realities we've discussed. But you are reading this book because you don't like where you are and you want your life to change. I've promised that I will tell you step-by-step how you can experience profound life change.

When you stop blaming others and start taking responsibility for the choices you make, you will get out of your pity pool and back into life. Perhaps you've been splashing about for a good long time, and you've grown quite comfortable where you are. Now that you've faced reality, you are ready to get out. The first think you must do if you are ready to stop playing in the tepid water of self-absorbed sadness is put your feet underneath you and exert the energy necessary to get up.

That might be easier said than done. I'm not young anymore, but I still love to exercise. My positive friend and trainer actually gives me a certain exercise that makes me wonder if he's preparing me for old age. Literally, for an exercise, he has me get up from lying on a mat to standing up—ten times in a row. This simple "exercise" actually requires more physical exertion than you might imagine. Brandon calls these exercises "get-ups."

Emotionally and spiritually speaking, to get up is to recognize that life is really hard, and God is really good, and you are really going to be okay. To get up is to say, "I'm done with *this* and ready for something else besides *this*."

Are you ready to get up?

The soldiers who serve our military take an oath when they join. They pledge their lives to protect the Constitution against enemies both at home and abroad. When our soldiers take this oath, they willingly place their lives under the authority of the President of the United States and the officers appointed over them. They place their confident trust in the regulations of the Uniform Code of Military Justice. The discipline of our military is absolutely necessary for our national security.

When we, the soldiers of the cross, take our oath, we willingly place our lives under the authority of Jesus Christ. We place our confident trust in the person and character of God as illustrated for us in His Word, the Bible. We have a Uniform Code of Military Justice in the perfect love and unblemished righteousness of our

Commander in Chief. Our discipline as soldiers of the cross is absolutely necessary for our spiritual security.

There were several times that Jesus's miracles attracted a crowd and when those crowds grew large, Jesus seized the opportunity to tell them just how difficult life might be if they chose to follow Him. Consider our call to follow: "Whoever wants to be my disciple, must deny themselves, take up their cross daily and follow Me" (Luke 9:23).

It would have been one thing had Jesus been speaking figuratively to His disciples, but not long after making this statement, He denied Himself, took up His cross, and followed His Father through what looked like madness but was rather the fulfillment of the most incredible plan ever.

Can you imagine what it might have been like to be one of Jesus's followers on the day of His crucifixion? Their hopes and dreams hung dying on that cross. There was nothing they could do to stop Him. They couldn't intervene when the soldiers came to arrest Him. Peter tried, and Jesus rebuked him as He replaced Malchus's ear. The men who'd given up their preconceived notions and dedicated themselves to realign their thinking to Jesus's teaching stood silent as Christ died. He told them that His death and resurrection were all a part of His Father's plan, but they had no context for understanding Him when He said that to them. Even when Jesus brought Lazarus back from the dead, and He said, "I am the resurrection and the life" (John 11:25). His disciples didn't understand. Would you have understood if you were them?

Perhaps you are stuck where you are because you don't understand. God has assured you that this terrible, awful thing can be woven into the fabric of "all things working together for good" (Romans 8:28), but this—*this*—can't possibly be woven into anything.

I would imagine Jesus's disciples felt the same way you feel when they stood in the shadow of the cross. Sometimes the space between Good Friday and Easter morning is incredibly long. The minutes that tick tock away between the horrible, no-good, very bad thing that happened to you and God's redemption of it may last a lifetime. So if you are living for Resurrection morning when the ache of Friday's crucifixion is finally redeemed, and if it's going to take a very long time for you to get there, you may miss the rest of your days on earth and leave your purpose unfulfilled. You can't just hold your breath and live for the day when your wrong is made right.

"Don't tell me that!" you might want to shout at me.

I know, it's awful! And many times, we do get to live to see God's better idea play out in our lives. He's always doing "exceedingly abundantly more than you can ask or imagine" and thank goodness we get to experience much of that activity. In fact, most of the time, we get to experience "Oh, now I get it!" Just like the disciples got to experience God's miraculous plan of the ages when they interacted with Jesus resurrected from the dead.

But every once in a while, we might bump up into something (or even more than one something) that isn't reconciled with our understanding of the goodness of God until we see Him face-to-face on the other side. And when this happens, we need to seek to understand God when He tells us what He's up to.

Jesus told His disciples the truth.

"As Jesus was going up to Jerusalem, he took the twelve disciples aside privately and told them what was going to happen to him. 'Listen,' he said, 'we are going up to Jerusalem, where the Son of Man will be betrayed to the leading priests and the teachers of religious law. They will sentence him to die. Then they will hand him over to the Romans to be mocked, flogged with a whip, and crucified. But on the third day he will be raised from the dead'" (Matthew 20:17–19 NLT).

Jesus explained exactly what was about to happen to Him. But when He was arrested, His disciples scattered. Had they understood what Jesus told them, they would not have had to endure the season of doubt, discouragement, and despair. Even if the disciples didn't understand that Jesus really would be raised from the dead, they could have chosen to acknowledge that their minds were limited, their thinking was faulty, and they still had much to learn about the incredible extent of God's power and His love.

This is the hard part. In order to *get up*, you must learn how to make your thoughts *bow down* to the lordship of Christ (II Corinthians 10:5). Here's how to do this:

1. Receive the truth when Jesus shares it with you.

Just as Jesus told His disciples the truth, Jesus tells you the truth too. The Bible is full of truth told from God's point of view and from His position when you are suffering. Here are a dozen truths that you can cling to in the dark:

"I am still confident of this; I will see the goodness of the Lord in the land of the living. Wait for the LORD; be strong and take heart and wait for the LORD." PSALM 145:13–14

"'Though the mountains be shaken and the hills be removed, yet my unfailing love for you will not be shaken nor my covenant of peace be removed,' says the LORD who has compassion on you." ISAIAH 54:10

"Forget the former things; do not dwell on the past. See, I am doing a new thing! Now it springs up; do you not perceive it? I am making a way in the desert and streams in the wasteland." ISAIAH 43:18–19

"But now, this is what the LORD says—He who created you, O Jacob, he who formed you, O Israel: 'Fear not, for I have redeemed you; I have summoned you by name; you are mine.'" ISAIAH 43:1

"I was young and now I am old. Yet I have never

seen the righteous forsaken or their children begging for bread." P<small>SALM</small> 37:25

"'Is not my word like fire,' declares the L<small>ORD</small>, 'and like a hammer that breaks a rock in pieces?'" J<small>EREMIAH</small> 23:29

"This is the confidence we have in approaching God; that if we ask anything according to his will, he hears us. And if we know that He hears us—whatever we ask—we know that we have what we asked of Him." I J<small>OHN</small> 5:14–15

"In my anguish I cried to the L<small>ORD</small> and he answered by setting me free." P<small>SALM</small> 118:5

"I was pushed back and about to fall, but the L<small>ORD</small> helped me. The L<small>ORD</small> is my strength and my song and has become my salvation." P<small>SALM</small> 118:13–14

"'The glory of this present house will be greater than the glory of the former house,' says the L<small>ORD</small> Almighty. 'And in this place I will grant peace,' declares the L<small>ORD</small> Almighty." H<small>AGGAI</small> 2:9

"Why are you downcast O my soul? Why so disturbed within me? Put your hope in God, for I will yet praise him, my Savior and my God." P<small>SALM</small> 43:5

"Shouts of joy and victory resound in the tents of

the righteous; the LORD*'s right hand has done mighty things!"* PSALM 118:15

These verses all speak to your spirit-woman. They tell you the truth. If you are having trouble believing what the Bible says, learn to recognize that God's Word is true and your point of view and position are often not. Part of living in a sin-stained world is contending with the filmy veil that sin creates to cloud and cloak what is and is not true.

The first church my husband and I attended as newlyweds and graduate students was pastored by a charismatic leader who often led the congregation to stand and make this public confession prior to his reading the Bible:

"I believe the Bible. It is the Word of God. Where what the Bible says differs from my beliefs, my attitudes, or my actions, I will change. By the power of God's Holy Spirit working in me. Amen."

This simple profession of faith identified a powerful truth we often forget. When the Bible says one thing and I believe something else, the Bible is right and I am wrong. Which leads to the next step to making your thoughts bow down to the lordship of Christ.

2. Let it be known that you are not capable of knowing all there is to know.

Consider this question: Could it be that because you've never experienced this before, you don't know all there is to know about it?

Your mind might not think right. My friend, you could even be wrong. Dare to entertain the possibility that you might not know enough about God, about life, and about spiritual realities to actually know what all is going on in your world. Much of our despair is created by our own vain imagination. We use our limited understanding to predict outcomes and cast judgment on people and circumstances. But we don't really know what all is going on!

And God does. The best thing about this truth is that our not knowing doesn't create God's not doing. God works all things together for your good and His glory. And only God can do this because only God knows what all is involved in the "all things" you are dealing with in your life. Only God knows the perfect timing when everything is in the right place. Scripture speaks often of the "fullness of time." God's timing isn't quick or slow; His timing is exactly right according to "all things" being in the right place at the right time for the right impact.

The Bible is full of promises that are for you. I shared a few of these just a minute ago. There are many more in there. At least one of those promises applies specifically to your circumstances. You have the incredible privilege of digging deep in God's Word as you search for the promise (or promises) that are yours. If you will be diligent to read God's Word on a daily basis, and invite Him to speak to you through it, you will discover the promises He has for you. And once you find the promises that are yours, know this: the power of these promises lies in this, God's Word is His bond.

"I bow before your holy Temple as I worship. I praise your name for your unfailing love and faithfulness; for your promises are backed by all the honor of your name." —Psalm 138:2 (NLT)

The very nature of God is at stake in the keeping of His Word. God will not lie to you. God will always tell you the truth. The Devil loves to keep you in your pity pool by heckling you with God's promises. He keeps you from standing up by mocking your faith. It's the nature of the Devil to mock the Word of the Lord.

"Did God say . . ?"

"God doesn't mean that! He . . ."

"If God's so good and this is what He's promised, then . . ."

Let me help you settle this battle here and now.

WHEN GOD GIVES YOU HIS WORD, HE WILL FULFILL IT.

I am a living witness to this fact. When my daughter Mikel left us just after high school graduation to live with the boyfriend we didn't want her to have, I initiated Post-It Note warfare in my home. Post-It Note warfare is simply claiming God's promises by printing them on yellow sticky notes and posting them all over your

home. Kaleigh (Mikel's sister, eighteen months young-
er) joined me in the fight and found Haggai 2:9.

*"'The glory of this present house will be greater than
the glory of the former house,' says the* LORD *Almighty.
'And in this place I will grant peace,' declares the* LORD
Almighty." —HAGGAI 2:9 (NIV)

When Kaleigh brought Haggai 2:9 on her yellow
sticky note, she said, "Mama, I don't know how on
earth God will ever create peace in our home and make
our family better than it has been in the past. I don't
know how we will ever be whole again, but this is the
word God gave me to claim."

It was a good word. But neither Kaleigh nor I had
the ability to comprehend how it would ever come
about. Our family was broken and we were hurting. We
thought we were a close-knit family and we'd had many
good times together, but we didn't think that even "all
the king's horses and all the king's men" could put our
family back together again. We smiled at one another,
took this yellow sticky note, and posted it on the wall
with the others.

Kaleigh and I had faith like a mustard seed. We didn't
sing and dance and celebrate God's promise, knowing
deep inside our spirits that now that He'd given us His
Word we could bank on Him to keep it. We just printed
Haggai 2:9 on a sticky note and begged Him to do
something great. On many occasions, the Devil mocked

me regarding that verse.

"You really think God's going to fix this?"

"It's been a year . . . three years . . . five . . . where's God? What's He up to?"

"Oh, now you've done it. Just when things were getting better you went and _____, maybe God was fixing it, but what do you think He's doing now?"

Or one of his best ways of messing with me was when I looked at old family photos. I had some hanging on the walls of my "laughing place." He used one picture in particular. It was taken Mikel's senior year in high school. My daughters and I wore white dresses, my son and husband had on white shirts and blue jeans. The kids held their dad in their arms while we all looked into the camera and laughed. That picture caught the spirit of our incredible family.

I would go to my "laughing place" to write and look at that picture, and Satan would whisper this, "Look at you then, before . . . you will never be like that again. I've taken what is precious to you, and God let me do it. Why would God do that to you? Why doesn't He answer your prayers?"

I could hardly look at that picture without hearing Haggai 2:9 echo in the distance of my heartbroken spirit.

Nevertheless, Kaleigh and I tried our best to "lean not on our own limited understanding" and instead to trust God and His Word. The less confidence we put in our understanding and the more confidence we determined to put in God, knowing more than we did, the more we were able to believe.

Kaleigh, whose faith is much more anchored in her ability to reason than in her ability to sense and feel, told me how she was winning this battle to believe. She pointed to Abraham. In Romans 4, you can read a fascinating retelling of Abraham's faith. Kaleigh especially picked up on this: "And being fully assured that what God had promised He is able also to perform" (Romans 4:21). One version of Scripture says that "Abraham reasoned in his heart." Kaleigh said that Abraham considered God; and in consideration of God's character, it was more likely that He would raise Isaac from the dead than that He would let Abraham's obedience negate God's promise.

Abraham didn't know all that was going on when he tied Isaac, his precious son, and his answered prayer to the altar, but He did know that God was a promise-keeper. And when Abraham clung to the promise of God, he found himself in a place where he was about to experience God like he'd never experienced Him before. Which is the third step to standing up by making your thoughts bow down.

1. Prepare to experience God like you've never experienced Him before.

When Jesus's disciples stood at the cross, their world shattered. Their Teacher, their Friend, their Counselor, Savior and Lord hung seemingly helpless and dying.

Their dreams were shattered and hope was gone. Just imagine what went through their minds when they lay down to sleep Friday night. I don't think they slept. I bet their minds were racing. They were beating themselves up for not stopping the madness. They were rethinking their actions, they were wishing for just one more conversation where they could tell Jesus how much they loved Him. They were sad and angry and confused and distraught and not certain what they would do in the morning.

But they were about to experience God like they had never experienced Him before. Out of all the miracles they'd been witnesses to, this was going to be the greatest one of all! The miracle of the resurrection was going to be the genuine expression of God's love and power—the plan of the ages was unfolding. All of God's activity in the past and all that He is yet to do in the future culminated with Jesus's resurrection from the dead.

Before the first Easter morning, Jesus's disciples had no context for understanding the extent of God's love or power. But when they saw Jesus resurrected from the dead—when Thomas put his hands in the scars on Jesus's side and palms—the disciples experienced God more. Before Jesus resurrected from the dead, the disciples knew God could calm a storm, feed five thousand, heal the sick, give sight to the blind, and cast demons out of tormented souls. They even knew He could raise the dead (to die again another day). After Jesus conquered the grave, the disciples knew that every word that came out of Jesus's mouth was true and that no matter how much the enemy seemed to have the upper hand, God would always be a step ahead.

You will know this too when you allow God to make sense of the madness in your own life. It's important to acknowledge that God's timing and yours may not be the same. It's important also to know that when you are learning something about God that you never knew before, everything that you did know before will most likely be challenged. But it's also important to remember that in time, you are going to think to yourself, "Why did I ever doubt Him?"

GET UP!

Are you ready to get up?

As a reminder: To get up is to recognize that life is really hard, and God is really good, and you are really going to be okay. To get up is to say, "I'm done with *this* and ready for something else besides *this*."

In order to get up, you teach your thoughts to bow down. Get up from where you're sitting and bow before the Lord (if you are physically able). Do these next three things on your knees as a physical expression of your willingness to submit yourself to God.

1. On your knees, receive the truth Jesus has for you.

Have you been claiming a particular verse from

Scripture? If so, print that verse in your journal. If not, consider that one of the twelve verses I shared with you in this chapter might be for you. Print that verse in your journal.

When you have a verse printed, read it aloud.

Now, pray this prayer. It is an adaptation of the confession our pastor invited us to make: *"Lord, I believe the Bible. It is Your Word. Where what the Bible says differs from my beliefs, my attitudes, or my actions, I will change. By the power of Your Holy Spirit working in me. I yield my mind, my heart, and my behavior to You. Change me. Amen."*

2. On your knees, confess that you are not capable of knowing all there is to know.

Have you ever noticed that after all of his suffering and all of his crying out through his crisis of belief, God never answered Job's complaint; instead, He asked Job some questions of His own. Most of God's questions followed the path of "Where were you when . . ?" And with those questions, God reminded Job that even though he knew a lot of things, he couldn't possibly know as much as God knew.

Job had a reasonable complaint before God—and most likely you do too. But even in this place of suffering, God's still God and you're still not. What you know is not all there is to know and what you don't know opens a world of possibility. The secret to opening that world of possibility is to confess that you don't know all there is to know.

Are you still on your knees? If not, get there now and pray with Job: *"I know that You can do anything and no one can stop You. You asked, 'Who is this that questions my wisdom with such ignorance?' It is I— and I was talking about things I knew nothing about, things far too wonderful for me.*

"You said, 'Listen and I will speak! I have some questions for You, and You must answer them.' I had only heard about You before, but now I have seen You with my own eyes. I take back everything I said, and I sit in dust and ashes to show my repentance." —Job 42:4–6 (NLT)

3. On your knees prepare to experience God like you've never experienced Him before.

Consider Jesus's prayer as He poured out His heart in the Garden of Gethsemane. Most likely, after His resurrection, Jesus told His disciples about His prayer (no one was awake to hear it when Jesus prayed). After begging God to let this cup of suffering pass from Him, Jesus prayed a tremendous prayer, *"Thy will be done."*

I want you to reflect on what we've discussed in this chapter and then pray this song. "Thy Will Be Done" by Hillary Scott. I like to use YouTube to watch the lyrics as I listen.

You get up when you bow down.

CHAPTER 5:

SHUT UP

In chapter 4, you learned that in order to get up, you must bow down. In this chapter, you are going to learn that in order to shut up, you are going to shout out.

I know, "shut up" was a bad word in our home when my children were growing up. But seriously, if you want to experience the freedom that comes your way when you stop blaming others and take responsibility for the choices you make, you will pay close attention to the tiny little tool between your teeth. I am going to go out on a limb and say, the words that come out of your mouth will either get you out of this place or keep you stuck where you are. I am going to take it one step further and say that the words that don't come out of your mouth—those that you use when you speak to yourself—will also get you out of this place or keep you stuck where you are.

Words are incredibly powerful!

I know you've most likely heard plenty about the negative power of our words; this chapter is not about that. Instead, we are going to talk about the incredible power you have to say anything—and how when you say the best things, the words that come out of your own mouth can and will work in your favor. If only we could take full control of our tongues. James said that if we could do that, we could control ourselves in every other way as well,

"For if we could control our tongues, we would be perfect and could also control ourselves in *every other way*" (James 4:2 NLT).

To think that if we could simply control what we say, we'd have the power to control ourselves in every other way! So, let's figure out how to shut up!

1. Listen to what you're saying.

Pay attention to what you're saying to others and to what you're saying to yourself. Listen to your words. Chances are, what's bubbling in your spirit is leaking out through your mouth. If you are feeling down, you most likely describe the clouds rather than the value of the rain. If you are feeling inadequate, unworthy, and insecure, you most likely reprimand yourself and demean your own value verbally. My sweet mother, who is the most amazing cook ever, was talking to herself last weekend in the kitchen where she was graciously cooking yummy meals for the pastors' wives at our retreat. "Lounette, you are making a mess of this. You can't do anything right this morning."

I heard her and was offended! She was talking about my amazing mother—who cooks better than anyone I know and who prepared and presented the best meals ever to those sweet women we wanted to bless. So I told her to hush. Her words weren't true, anyway.

Diane, the gracious wife of a seminary professor who loves pastors' wives so much that she spends her life ministering to them, was hosting this retreat. Out of her tenacious fundraising, Diane was able to fully fund an incredible weekend for ministers' wives who couldn't have participated in this weekend away if they had been responsible for funding their own way. Several times, I heard Diane say that she was not a good fundraiser. And yet, she'd paid for the entire weekend! I doubted her words.

Then we went out shopping one afternoon in nearby Blowing Rock, North Carolina, and Diane chatted with one of the shopkeepers. I'd met Penny before and we'd talked about the remodel she and her husband did to their old farmhouse. But when Diane met Penny, I discovered that Penny was a Christian author and speaker who led a ministry to women. I also discovered that Penny was my neighbor! After we talked with Penny for nearly an hour, we left her shop and I told Diane to stop saying she wasn't a good fundraiser. I reminded her that fundraising is networking and her networking skills are incredible.

Listen to what you are saying to yourself, to others about yourself, and even in general. Pay close attention to the words that just tumble out of your mouth without much thought. Sometimes we carefully weigh our words and at other times, we just let them roll. Pay attention to those rolling words especially.

2. Change what you're hearing.

What might happen to the way my mom and Diane feel when they are up to their earlobes in biscuit dough and ministry if they spoke honest words of encouragement to themselves? My mom might say something like this, "Now, Lounette, you know you can do this! You've done it a hundred times before. Let's get 'er done!" And Diane might say, "I have a call on my life and know beyond a shadow of a doubt that He who began a good work in me will be faithful to complete it! Where I am weak, He is strong and by the power of the Holy Spirit working in me, I will connect with the hearts of men and women who have money to share. They will be happy to share it, and these women will be blessed to receive it."

Now, I'm neither a fundraiser nor am I a cook. But I can write a book, and I know that my books are easier to write when I encourage myself than they are when I am hard on myself. David knew his words were powerful so David spoke forth encouragement. Read Psalm 139:13–18. In these words, David talked about himself in a way that was true, positive, and directed toward God.

For you formed my inward parts;
you knitted me together in my mother's womb.
14 *I praise you, for I am fearfully and wonderfully*
made.[a]
Wonderful are your works;
my soul knows it very well.
15 *My frame was not hidden from you,*
when I was being made in secret,
intricately woven in the depths of the earth.
16 *Your eyes saw my unformed substance;*
in your book were written, every one of them,
the days that were formed for me,
when as yet there was none of them.
17 *How precious to me are your thoughts, O God!*
How vast is the sum of them!
18 *If I would count them, they are more than the sand.*
I awake, and I am still with you. (ESV)

If we were to walk about daily marveling in the intricate details of the human body, and the marvelous gift of life, we might be less inclined to camp out on our shortcomings and instead shout out loud, "I praise You, Lord! For I am fearfully and wonderfully made!"

In fact, it would do you good to do that right now! Shout it out!

"I am fearfully and wonderfully made!
Your works are wonderful, Lord, I know this well!"

3. Be intentional about what you say, when you say it, how you say it, and what you choose not to say.

One Wednesday night, my friend Barb presented a study on the power of the tongue. Proverbs 18:21 was the basis of her message. Here's a picture of her chalkboard where she wrote the words:

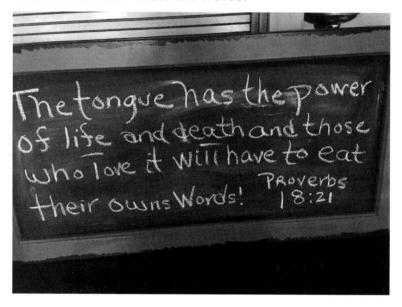

Barb went to a local slaughterhouse (yes, we live in the country) where she asked the butcher for a cow's tongue. She took that tongue and placed it in a gallon-sized plastic bag, and then put it in a large paper grocery sack. For an icebreaker activity, Barb took the bag around the room and invited the women to reach in, feel the tongue, and guess what they were feeling.

As you can well imagine, this "feel what's in my

bag" created quite a stir. Barb told me this, "I then gave them a hint that it was a weapon that we could use but very hard to control or handle. I spoke about things we have said to our husbands and friends and family that we can't take back. I shared that out of the heart the mouth speaks and that changing your heart is the answer to controlling your tongue." Barb went on to say that she's literally taught women to bite their tongue instead of speaking harmful and hurtful things.

I wasn't at the study that night, but Barb's object lesson left quite the impression on the women who were there. The tongue is a powerful weapon that is hard to control and when you learn to control your tongue, when you learn to tame your tongue, when you learn to use your ability to speak positive words, you will be amazed at how quickly your feelings will follow your words.

As I write this chapter, I'm sitting at a local bakery/ coffee shop waiting for two friends to arrive. They are friends from many years ago and although we live in the same community, our paths no longer cross. One is a college professor, the other is a full-time author and speaker. They both had preschoolers when my children were preschoolers and we all went to church together.

They are squeezing me into their busy lives this afternoon because I felt like there was something I needed to tell them. Because of how full our schedules are, they suggested I just say what I had to say through a Facebook message. I tried to write what I wanted to tell them, but it didn't come out the way I wanted to say it.

I actually want to apologize to them for something that happened a long time ago. I need to see their faces when I'm sharing what I have to say. I can't fully express the depth of my remorse in writing.

We met, and our time together was good. In this day when there are so many ways to communicate without talking face-to-face with one another, we sometimes miss the gift of sincere exchange of thoughts and feelings. My friends were gracious, and there was healing in our connecting face-to-face.

We have much power in our choice of words, in the inflection of our voices, and the passion in which we deliver them. Our little tongues can build up or tear down. With our words, we can encourage our loved ones to become more than they might ever imagine. We can also hinder them in ways we'd never imagine. We do the same to ourselves.

TAME YOUR TONGUE STEP-BY-STEP

We are going to attempt to do the impossible. With these steps, you are going to tame your powerful tongue.

Step 1: Think on these things.

Scripture gives us many directives related to taming our tongues. One of my favorite verses is Philippians 4:8.

"Finally brothers and sisters, whatever is true, whatever is noble, whatever is right, whatever is pure, whatever is lovely, whatever is admirable, if anything is excellent or praiseworthy think on these things."

If you are thinking on the things that are true, noble, right, pure, lovely, admirable, excellent, and praiseworthy, you will talk about these things. Whatever is on your mind is certain to find its way out of your mouth. So, what you think will determine what you say.

Rather than break this verse into bits, use the descriptive words all together to direct your attention in the circumstances of your life. For instance, say you get sick (I got sick writing this chapter), and you have a fever and feel terrible. You could dwell on the sickness itself, or the things you can't get done while you are sick or any number of things that are not excellent or praiseworthy. Or you could think on the fact that if you have to be sick in August, you get to be sick in an air-conditioned house, and your daughter makes the best iced tea in the world, and that tea nurses you through the worst of your illness.

Think on the things that are excellent and praiseworthy. A great place to start is to ask yourself this one simple question: What is good about this? Learn to look from any angle that allows you to see something good. Even if the best thing about a situation is this: "This is one day, praise God, I will never have to live again."

Step 2: Fill your heart with what is good.

Jesus said, "The mouth speaks what the heart is full of." Some people have learned to do what Barb encouraged the women to do: "Bite your tongue." And until you can deal with the heart of the issue, some tongue-biting might be great advice. But consider how much easier it is to have your heart filled with good things so that your mouth automatically spills these things out on others.

So how do we fill our hearts with good things?

The doorway to the heart is the mind. The thoughts you think will lead to the feelings and attitudes you carry in your heart. So, think good thoughts! Train your brain to think on the things that are true, noble, pure, lovely, admirable, excellent, and praiseworthy.

This is why step 2 comes after step 1. Once you begin to train your brain to think good thoughts, you will begin to notice that your heart is filling with good things. Notice that I have said nothing about changing your circumstances or what other people do to you. I am talking simply about changing your perspective. You might need to change your circumstances and separate yourself from harmful people—we will talk about that in a bit.

Here are some practical things you can do. Smile at people. Wave at them when you pass them on the road. Greet strangers even, and be the kind of person who makes someone else's day brighter. Wear cheerful colors and carry an audaciously big purse. It's hard to be sullen when you're carrying a big purse, especially when you fill it with the things that make you happy. Things like chocolate! (Only not in August when you have no air conditioning.)

Step 3: Cultivate an attitude of gratitude.

A great way to engage your heart is to cultivate an attitude of gratitude. I cannot say enough about the difference a grateful heart will make as you seek to tame your tongue. My son is a motivational speaker. He delivers his messages via YouTube. If you want to be inspired to cultivate an attitude of gratitude and like the perspective of a twenty-one-year-old, take a look at his video https://www.youtube.com/watch?v=e_H774ds8Nc.

We all have things to be grateful for! TJ challenges us to find three things to be thankful for no matter what we are facing. A person you love; something mundane (you take for granted); and something physical. When you actively look for things to be thankful for, you are focusing on things that are good. And, TJ is right: when you actually feel grateful, you cannot feel any other way. You can't feel grateful and feel depressed. You can't feel grateful and feel mad. You can't feel grateful and feel discouraged. So when you choose to be grateful, when you decide to count your blessings, you will feel better!

Take a look at Romans 1:21 (NIV): "For although they knew God, they neither glorified him as God nor gave thanks to him, but their thinking became futile and their foolish hearts were darkened."

Don't be like them. You know God! Glorify Him as God and give Him thanks for the miracle of life, for the sun that rises and then sets. Praise Him that when you go to sleep, you wake up again. Glorify God for creating the perfect conditions to sustain life on earth. Praise Him in the morning and praise Him in the evening. Praise Him when the sun goes down.

A great way to cultivate an attitude of gratitude is to consider three things for which you are grateful every morning before you get out of bed. Then, when you are having your quiet time, make a list of ten more things. Before every meal, include three things you are grateful for in your blessing. And before you go to bed at night, thank God for one thing that happened that day for which you are grateful. Just the practice of training your brain to think these thoughts will lead you toward filling your heart with good things and when your heart is full of good things, your mouth will speak of them. And when your mouth speaks of good things, you will be well on your way to getting out of your pity pool and taking personal responsibility for yourself. As you take responsibility for yourself, you will learn that you have a whole lot more power over the circumstances of your life and the feelings in your heart than you thought you had before.

SHUT UP!

In this chapter, we've discussed three things you can do to get well on your way out of the pity pool.

1. Listen to what you're saying.
2. Change what you're hearing.
3. Be intentional about what you say, when you

say it, how you say it, and what you choose not to say.

I then mapped out a plan for you to accomplish these three things.

1. Think on the Philippians 4:8 things.
2. Fill your heart with what is good.
3. Cultivate an attitude of gratitude.

These three things are what you, and only you, can do. They are not dependent on what anyone else does or doesn't do. You have the power to change your life this very minute by taming your tongue. And you can do it!

Although this has been a practical, step-by-step kind of chapter, I still want to wrap it up by giving you a practical application of what I've presented.

1. Memorize Philippians 4:8.
2. Take time daily to list at least one thing that is true, noble, right, pure, lovely, admirable, excellent, and praiseworthy. Collect those things!
3. Pay attention to the things you think that you *don't* think about by engaging in conversation with your thoughts. Dismiss the things you think that are not Philippians 4:8 approved.
4. Insert these power words into your daily

conversations: "I'm proud of you!" "I love you." "I missed you." "I'm grateful for you."

I dare you to do these things. When you do, you will find the pity pool much less inviting and the way out much more enticing. So maybe the title of this chapter should be "Shout Out" rather than "Shut Up." Shout out the good stuff; those things—those things that are true, noble, right, pure, lovely, admirable, excellent, and praiseworthy.

CHAPTER 6:

DO NOT BE DECEIVED

I've promised to get you out of your pity pool by empowering you to stop blaming others and take full responsibility for the choices you make. So far, I've challenged you to embrace some of life's realities; to stand up by bowing down (under the lordship of Christ); and then I just flat out told you to shut up. And I know, that wasn't nice. But it really turned into an exhortation to shout out. And that's not so bad.

Now, I want to encourage you to step out. Consider how long a toddler toddles about before she takes her first step. I find it fascinating that toddlers "cruise" for weeks before they are confident enough to let go and step out. I hope that you don't spend weeks cruising, but if you do, that's better than splashing; so even if you don't think you're quite ready for the next step, humor me and read on.

Because stepping out is such a big deal, we are going to take several chapters to unpack the necessary thought processes you need to go through to not only take your first step, but to keep on walking. In these next few chapters, we are going to discuss a very real adversary (the Devil) who wants to keep you right where you are. Then we're going to camp out in Romans 8:26–39 until we are saturated in the incredible truths we find there.

THE DEVIL SPINS A WICKED WEB

I'm not sure how you feel about spiritual warfare, but Scripture teaches us that it's real. The powers of spiritual darkness have been active in your life already whether you credited them with the activity or not. I've written two books on the subject of spiritual warfare, and in all my research regarding the ways of the Devil, the one thing I know to be true every time is that Satan loves to exercise the power of deception. In my book, *Spiritual Warfare for Your Family*, I explain why he operates this way. It has to do with the fact that he's been soundly defeated and is outnumbered two-to-one. In this chapter, I'm going to explain what deception is and give you a few illustrations of the Devil's use of it so that you can get yourself untangled from his wicked web.

The definition of *deception* is "to trick someone into believing something that is not true." The wickedness of deception is that the victim *believes* he is right when he is wrong. Several years ago, I believed many things to be true. I had spiritual formulas. You most likely have them too. They were formulas for success, and formulas for love, and formulas for healthy friendships, and formulas for staying out of trouble. Each of my formulas went something like this: "If I do *thus and so*, then God will do *this and that*." My formulas were based on biblical truth. For instance, I believed that if I reared my children in church, read Bible stories to them at night, taught them how to have a quiet time, and prayed for them daily, if I led them to Christ and lived the Christian life in front of them, then God would watch over them when I could not and keep them out of trouble. The Devil deceived me into believing that he would leave my kids alone just because I loved them greatly and did my part to lead them toward the Lord. I learned that I could do all those things, and my children still had the opportunity to choose for themselves whether or not they would live their lives in relationship with God. I could do all those things and the Devil still lurked about in the shadows of their Christian school, and in the corners of my home, seeking to devour them.

I didn't know I was being deceived until I came face-to-face with a God I didn't understand; One who seemed to be less than concerned about my welfare; a God who let me down, disappointed me, and remained silent when I shouted out to Him in my despair. It wasn't until my faith failed me that I re-examined it and began to build a faith that never fails. Through that dark and difficult journey, I learned that a faith that never fails is a faith that understands the Devil is a deceiver.

THE DEVIL USES SCRIPTURE TO DECEIVE YOU

The Devil loves to take biblical principles and redirect them so that they become me-centered rather than

God-centered. Consider these biblical principles and the Devil's distortion of them:

1. "For I know the plans I have for you," declares the LORD, "they are plans to prosper you and not to harm you, to give you hope and a future" (Jeremiah 29:11 NIV).

   Satan interprets this verse for you, "God's got good plans for your life. He will prosper you so that you will never be hurt, wounded, or broken-hearted. God is obligated to give you good things and not bad things from now until the day you die."

   But then something terrible happens and Satan's right there to offer his condolences. "How can this possibly be good for you? What kind of God would allow this to happen in your life? What's the matter with Him?"

   First, Satan twists the truth to set you up for God to let you down and then he comes along and accuses God of being less than who He claims to be.

2. "Ask and it will be given to you, seek and you will find, knock and the door will be opened to you" (Matthew 7:7 NIV).

   Satan interprets this verse for you, "God's supposed to answer your prayers! So, go ahead, ask Him anything!" And Satan's "anything" might be earthly power and riches, popularity for your kids, even success for their ball teams! (I mean, I prayed for my batters when they were standing at home plate, and for my fielder when she was out in center field. I prayed for my basketball player to make his free throws!) God said to ask for *anything!*

Then when you pray your heart out, and still don't receive the answer you're looking for, Satan heckles you, "What's the matter? Keep on asking! God won't answer you? Something must be wrong with you." Or, "Something must be wrong with God."

3. And then there's the classic one we love to quote when things aren't going so well, "And we know that all things work together for good to them that love God, to them who are the called according to *his* purpose" (Romans 8:28 KJV).

Satan's interpretation, "It's all good! Everything's going to be okay. God's obligated to work it out for you. He's got this! Don't worry, it's all good."

Then when you spend a few days, months, or even years holding your breath and waiting for the good to come, Satan hangs in there with you. "What's happened to God? Where did He go? How can He let this happen to you?"

Notice that in all these verses, you are given a truth to cling to. Satan takes hold of that truth and distorts it. His subtle distortion comes in the form of shifting your focus from a God-centered life to a self-centered life. Satan's lie is that you know better than God how to rule your world. Satan's lie is that you know better than God how to navigate this sin-stained world in such a way that you come out on top. He taps in to your sin-sensitive bent to rebel against authority and protect your *self*.

Isn't this the root of the blame game? Don't we blame others for our own discomfort and misfortune because we believe, deep down, that we deserve better than the way they are treating us?

Whenever Satan can convince you that *you*, rather than God, deserve to sit on the throne in your life, he is able to deceive you, even with Scripture.

THE DEVIL USES THE THINGS OF THIS WORLD TO DECEIVE YOU

Another aspect of Satan's deception is to maneuver you away from the "glorious riches" God has given you, and convince you to exchange them for the temporal things of this world (that he rules). He has your flesh, and your biological connection to this world to trip you up.

Here is a simple example of how this deception works. You might enjoy a cup of coffee to get your day started and a glass of wine to relax when the day is done.

Coffee and wine are not the sin, but if you develop a dependence on the chemical reaction your body has with these substances, and the coffee and wine take the place of your dependence on God, then you have exchanged the things of the spirit for the things of the world.

Let's leave coffee and wine alone and exchange it for working out and eating right. Those are great things to do for your physical body and the endorphins they create overflow into your spirit. But I've seen good people dedicate themselves to working out and eating right and neglecting their time with the Lord. I've seen them indulge so much in body sculpting that they never noticed when they crossed over the moral lines God set for their own safety and literally wrecked their lives.

When you fulfill a spiritual need with a physical pseudo substitute, you trick your spirit into being satisfied by the flesh. Flesh can never satisfy the spirit. Flesh is like a weed that grows and grows and chokes out the fruitfulness of your spirit. When you choose to go with God, you give Him first place in your life. When you give God first place in your life, you make flesh and sin leave the throne room altogether.

Jesus understood the power of the flesh, and this is why He made some drastic and hard-to-understand statements:

> "Whoever wants to be my disciple must deny themselves and take up their cross daily and follow me" (Luke 9:23).

And then He went on to say,

> "For whoever wants to save their life will lose it, but whoever loses their life for me will save it" (Luke 9:24).

I've already mentioned that I would like to have thought that Jesus was speaking figuratively when He made those statements. But you and I both know that Jesus never asked anything of His disciples that He was not willing to do Himself. He denied himself, took up His cross, and followed His Father all the way through crucifixion and death. You cannot cling to a "happily ever after" life pursuit and go with Jesus too. If you want to go with Jesus, you must deny yourself, take up your cross, and follow Him.

Life on earth, with its pleasures and happiness, success and accolades, matters only if life on earth is all that we have. If heaven is real and eternity is our destination, wouldn't it make sense to give up all the pleasures of this life? If heaven is real, the best that this life has to deliver is still merely a blip on the screen of eternity. When Jesus invited us to follow Him, He told us that the sacrifice would be worth it. He told us that there is a much greater life; a much greater reality; a much greater existence on the other side of death. We prove that we believe Him when we choose to give our life over to Him. This reminds me of a phrase in one of the songs we sang when I was young, *"And the things of life will grow strangely dim in the light of His glory and grace."*

THE DEVIL USES OFFENSE TO DECEIVE YOU

It is impossible to go through life without having someone offend you. And often it seems that those who deliver the injustice to you actually get away with it. If you've ever been taken to court, or if you've ever taken someone else to court, you know that even our justice system is not sufficient to really serve us "justice." Cases are "settled" all the time by convincing two parties to come to an agreement. Often those agreements allow the offending party to get away with at least some of their wrong behavior.

We have an innate desire to be vindicated when someone does us wrong. But often, people seemingly get away with their wrong behavior and we are left to deal with the tragic results of their actions. Satan loves to spin much of his web around the sticky issue of offense.

Satan has several lies that serve his purposes when you come up against an offense.

Lie #1: You do not deserve to be treated that way.
  How dare they do that to you!
Lie #2: You can make them pay for that!
Lie #3: If you get them back, you will feel better.

The Devil loves to come alongside us and lend us

comfort when we are offended. Oh, Satan is like Florence Nightingale when it comes to tending to our offenses. "Can you believe what just happened to you? I can't believe it! Oh my goodness! Let me help you!" And then he proceeds to carefully examine the pain you are feeling. Only the nursing of an offense will not heal the pain but rather transform it into a grudge. And nursing a grudge will only cause it to become an unpleasant companion that insists on going wherever you go and making himself known whenever he goes there.

Bitterness replaces joy. Jesus told us exactly how to combat Satan's attempt to derail us with bitterness.

"But I say to you, love your enemies and pray for those who persecute you, so that you may be sons of your Father who is in heaven; for He causes His sun to rise on *the* evil and *the* good, and sends rain on *the* righteous and *the* unrighteous. For if you love those who love you, what reward do you have? Do not even the tax collectors do the same? If you greet only your brothers, what more are you doing *than others?* Do not even the Gentiles do the same?" —Matthew 5:44–47 (NASB).

Jesus tells us how to deflect Satan's fiery dart when he loads it with the poison of bitterness. Refuse to nurse that grudge. Don't replay the offense over and over in your mind. Don't reread the message, don't retell the story, just don't dwell on it at all! Take your hurt feelings and lay them at the foot of the cross where your own sin crucified your Savior.

But Jesus didn't stop there. He said to love your enemies! Pray for them! And when good things happen as a result of your prayers, be glad. I don't know about you, but that doesn't come naturally to me. I kind of want my spiritual formulas to work in reverse. If I do the right things, I want God to give me the good things and if they do the wrong things, I want God to give them the bad things. It's natural to feel this way; it might not be natural to admit feeling this way, but it doesn't take any effort at all to wish for my enemies to be reprimanded or disciplined or to get warts on the ends of their noses.

So once again, you have to decide if you are going to live for self or live for Christ. Sometimes my children challenged me when I directed their paths. They challenged me with this question, "Why?" And they asked it in the whiniest of tones. It's the exact kind of challenge I'd like to present to Jesus when I'm offended and He tells me to love my offender and to pray for them. "Why?"

Do you know how I answered my children when they whined that question to me? "Because I said so, that's why!"

Now I always had my reasons, but the tone of their voice gave me an indication that no matter what my reasons were, they were not interested in doing what I asked them to do. I wonder how many times I am like a child. How many times do I whine at God from my position of limited experience and shortsighted understanding and balk at His instructions? In this case, a firm, "Because I said so!" should be enough. For when we refuse to deflect the fiery dart full of poisonous bitterness, we suffer greatly. And sometimes time is of the essence.

THE DEVIL'S HOOK

Satan is always looking for ways to deceive you. His hook is your desire to be master of your own life. As long as you are seeking happiness and fulfillment in the things of this world—as long as you are pursuing self-preservation and an easier way—your faith will be challenged and most likely defeated. It's only when you choose to seek first His Kingdom and His righteousness that "all these things will be added unto you" (Matthew 6:33).

Satan rules this world by default. Adam and Eve gave him control when they disobeyed God. He's smart, he's wicked, and he's well versed in the nature of mankind. He knows where you are weak and he knows how to trigger your doubt. He weaves a wicked web of deception and can cause really good people to do really bad things even to one another. But you have the power to utterly disarm him when you place your complete hope, confidence, and trust in God.

I had a friend relay this story to me regarding Henrietta Mears. Henrietta was a Christian educator who served many years at Hollywood's First Presbyterian Church. She is attributed to having created the first Sunday school, and her life impacted the lives of Bill Bright (Campus Crusade for Christ) and Billy Graham (evangelist). At the end of her life, some of her friends asked her, "What would you do differently?" And she responded, "I would trust Him more."

I cannot imagine how a woman like Henrietta, whose life produced so much fruit for the kingdom, could have trusted Him any more. But I do know that I can certainly "trust Him more" in my life. There are so many times I want to cry out, "This isn't fair!" or "Why me?" or "Why?" in a whiny tone and argumentative spirit. Most often, God remains silent and in due season, I understand more. If only I could follow Him when I don't understand, and choose Him when I can't comprehend, and trust Him more every step of the way.

OVERCOME THE DEVIL'S DECEPTION

You can defeat him, you know. The Devil's powerful, but he's not as powerful as God. And when you walk with the Lord, you walk in His strength and power and the Devil doesn't stand a chance against God. Here is something practical you can do right now to overcome the Devil's deception.

1. Choose to believe that God's Word is true.

We will talk more about this in the next chapter. But for now, begin to search Scripture that counters Satan's deception. Consider taking the three verses I mentioned previously—those three that Satan loves to distort—Jeremiah 29:11, Matthew 7:7, and Romans 8:28. Print each verse on a piece of paper. In your quiet time, answer these questions for each verse (use the Internet for your research).

- What is the context in which this verse was first spoken? For instance, Jeremiah 29:11 was given to the prophet Jeremiah regarding Israel's captivity and eventual freedom from captivity. Look into the life and culture of the people who wrote these verses so that you will gain a better understanding of what they mean.
- Is there or has there ever been a time when God allowed something and even though you thought it was going to be bad, it turned out to be good? If so, how does that impact the message given in these verses?
- Will this verse stand the test of time? Does it reach into eternity?

2. Take account of your worldly affections.

Consider giving up one or more of them for a specific period of time. This is called a "fast." When you separate yourself from connection to this world, you give your spirit room to grow. God will meet you in special ways when you fast. You might consider fasting from food, beverages, shopping, social media, television; the list could go on and on. When you participate in your fast, listen for God's voice and record what you hear.

3. Are you ready for number 3? Let go of your offenses.

- Does that mean they might get away with being mean to you? Yes.
- Does that mean you might never get back what you lost? Perhaps.
- Does that mean you can't invite others to understand how they made you feel? Yes.
- Do I have to? No. You can choose not to, but if you will let go of your offenses, you will be free to step out of your pity pool. Guaranteed.

I love doing something tangible so that I can hold on to the experience when I'm tempted to doubt my resolve. Consider writing your offenses on separate pieces of paper and burning them in a fire. It might be a good idea to host a personal offense burning periodically if you get your feelings hurt easily. Just think how free you can be when you choose to simply *let it go!*

The Devil does spin a wicked web, but if you choose to trust God more, if you discipline yourself by separating yourself from the world for a period of time, and if you keep a very short list of those who've offended you (so short, in fact, that there's not room for even a name), then you will discover how to free yourself from his web of deception.

CHAPTER 7:

KNOW GOD WORKS

I was diagnosed with colon cancer, it recurred in my liver two years later, and I refused the steroids that accompanied the chemo treatments so I was physically sicker than I had to be. But in the midst of that, I was fighting a spiritual battle for my daughter that seemed to heckle everything I'd ever believed about God and His Word. All the while, I wrote books. It might have been my therapy. One day, I received a box in the mail, and it was filled with Lifeway Christian Resources new women's Bible studies (a perk of my service as a trainer for them), and at the bottom of the box, there was a plaque: "All things work together for good TO THEM THAT LOVE GOD" Romans 8:28.

I held it in my hands and wept.

I was sick and I was tired and my faith was worn thin. I was trying hard to "trust Him more" and just when I needed to be reminded, God sent me His word.

"All things work together for good."

Those words echoed in my heart and my head. I

wrote a message based on that verse and I'm going to share it here. There are three points I'm going to make in regards to applicable truths we can gain from Romans 8:28. I'm going to show those points to you in the story of Martha and Mary when Jesus let Lazarus die before He responded to their desperate request for Him to come to their rescue. You can read the story in John 11.

1. Romans 8:28 is a promise written for those who love God and are called according to His purpose.

I still think it's interesting that the plaque I received only quoted a portion of Romans 8:28, and it emphasized this part of the verse, "All things work together for good TO THEM THAT LOVE GOD." I liked that. It was like a reassuring pat on my spiritual bottom (that's what the guys do) to say, "Hey, Leighann, you're going to be okay, because God's already assured you that He's working this out. You get to claim this verse because you love Him!"

In relationship to Martha and Mary, they too could claim this verse because they had a personal relationship with Jesus. As their story unfolds in John 11, we read that Mary was the one who poured expensive perfume on the Lord's feet and wiped them with her hair. And that when she and Martha sent their message to Jesus, they referred to their brother as Jesus's "dear friend." One translation calls Lazarus, "the one that you love" (John 11:1–3).

Mary, Martha, and Lazarus were qualified to claim Romans 8:28 as their own personal promise because they were three of Jesus's closest friends. They were "those who love God and are called according to His purpose for them." Mary, Martha, and Lazarus didn't just know about Jesus. They *knew* Him! They ate with Him, and they interacted with him. They shared their hearts and their lives and their dreams with Him. They were intimately acquainted with Him.

Because of their personal relationship with Jesus, Martha and Mary knew that Jesus loved them *and* that He had the power to fix whatever was wrong with them. They knew He would want to know if something was desperately wrong. They just knew that He would want to respond to them in their hour of need.

They were just like you!

They were just like me!

But not only did Martha, Mary, and Lazarus love Jesus, Jesus loved them right back. In John 11:5, we read this,

"Jesus loved Martha, Mary, and Lazarus . . ."

Are you qualified to claim Romans 8:28 for yourself? Do you know of God or do you know God? Does your life illustrate your love for Him? If I were to observe your life over the course of this next week, how would I know that you loved Jesus? Jesus said in John 15:14 that those who love Him will obey His commands.

"You are my friends if you do what I command."

We come into a personal relationship with God

through the generous gift of salvation. There's nothing we bring to the table—in terms of our salvation—except for the sin that nailed Jesus to the cross. Salvation is a free gift. God freely gave His Son.

When we receive God's gift of salvation, we enter into a personal relationship with God that changes everything. We become a follower of Christ, a believer in Him, a Christian or Christlike person. We don't earn our salvation by obedience to God's Word—we prove it that way.

Several years back, I swam on the Master's Swim Team. I know, the name sounds fancy, but really the Master's Swim Team just means that if you are a grown-up and you show up, you can be a member of the team. I didn't have to swim to be on the team, but rather I swam because I was on the team. In the same way, we don't obey God to be saved; we obey Him because we are saved.

Not only do we prove our salvation by being obedient to God's Word, but if we have a relationship with God, it will be intimate and personal as opposed to general and impersonal. My husband pastors a large church. For many people, he is their pastor. They know him and many of them are known by him. But, friends, I *know* Tom McCoy. He's my husband, and he loves the people in his church, but there's not a soul on this planet that Tom McCoy loves more than me. I know him like you don't know him. We do all of life together and we are intimately acquainted with one another. This is the kind of intimate companionship and knowledge and living-life-together that God wants us to experience with Him.

Just showing up for church on Sunday is not going to get you closer to God. Even working for God in the church or in the world is not going to get you to the place of intimacy God offers you. If you want to experience the truth of Romans 8:28 in your life, then be like Martha, Mary, and Lazarus. Be intimately acquainted with Jesus. Spend time with God in His Word. Learn how to hear His voice, obey His commands, and invite His presence into the "all things" in your life.

2. Romans 8:28 challenges us to hear the truth God speaks in His Word.

In John 11:4, we are told the truth:

"But when Jesus heard about it he said, 'Lazarus' sickness will not end in death. No, it happened for the glory of God so that the Son of God will receive glory from this.'"

Note carefully what Jesus said, "Lazarus' sickness will not end in death." Jesus didn't actually say that Lazarus would not die. He said that death would not be the end of Lazarus. But what the disciples heard Jesus say was this, "We don't have to leave just yet, because Lazarus isn't going to die."

Have you ever misheard the voice of God? Did your own limited faith stifle the possibilities of what God's power could do and therefore cause you to hear something God never said? Several times in my life, I've come face-to-face with this reality in communication. I think I said one thing and the other person heard something completely different than what I thought I had said.

Does that ever happen to you? I've come to the conclusion that often my brain muffles my ears. My thoughts get ahead of my sense of hearing, and sometimes, if I'm not careful, I truly am processing thoughts that are anchored in what I thought I heard, but those words were never actually said. I hear what I want to hear—or what I don't want to hear—and completely miss the actual words that were being spoken. This can cause problems indeed!

Often, Romans 8:28 heckles us because of this hearing issue. We have assumed that we know better than God what is and what is not good. And then we proceed to enlighten Him! This happens when we pray and expect God to listen to us. We approach His throne of grace boldly and proceed to tell Him not only what needs to be fixed, but also how He ought to fix it. It's as if we expect God to report to us each morning in order to find out what He needs to be doing that day.

Consider these truths:

God is never taken by surprise.

God is never making things up as he goes along or adjusting His plans because of unexpected developments.

God knows what He's up to even when you don't.

And most of the time, God tells you what He's up to even though you aren't listening! Your own lack of faith serves as a barrier between you and confident expectation of God's greater things for your life.

Ask God to give you ears to hear, eyes to see, a mind to imagine, and a heart to believe that absolutely *nothing* is impossible for Him (Luke 1:37). Ask Him to consistently remind you that whatever you can ask or imagine, He's going to do better than that (Eph. 3:20). Then you can live victoriously through the "meantime" where what God has promised and what you are experiencing are two very different things.

3. Romans 8:28 increases our faith.

Martha and Mary just *knew* that if they let Jesus know their problem, He would come to their rescue. I imagine that they assumed He would come right away. For Jesus loved Martha, Mary, and Lazarus! When John 11 begins, Martha and Mary trusted Jesus with the life of their brother—even though he was critically ill. They were understandably disappointed when Lazarus died and Jesus never came.

Can you imagine how they might have felt? It had to take some time to deliver their message to Jesus, then Jesus stayed put for a few days, and then it had to take some time for Jesus to travel back to them. When He finally arrived, they told Him that Lazarus had been dead for four days. Four long days of silence from God. Four long days of unimaginable grief and suffering brought about by sickness and death. No wonder Martha greeted Jesus this way: "If only you had been here, Jesus! Our brother wouldn't have died!" (John 11:21). And then Mary greeted Him the exact same way: "Lord, if only you had been here, my brother wouldn't have died" (John 11:32).

Have you ever fallen at the feet of Jesus with an "If only?" If only you had come to my rescue! If only you had answered my prayers! If only you had given me better discernment! If only . . . and the list could go on and on and on. It's these "if only" times in our lives when Romans 8:28 becomes either a slap in the face or an anchor for our storm-tossed souls.

The waves come crashing in the form of questions:

Does God really mean what He says in Romans 8:28?

And if He does, why do such terrible things happen in our lives?

Why doesn't Jesus come when we call Him?

Why doesn't He respond to our prayers?

Why, if He loves us and we love Him, can't we count on Him to do what we reasonably expect Him to do?

Why doesn't He intervene in the midst of these terrible things and why doesn't He stop them from getting worse?

Don't forget that God *always* tells us the truth in His Word. And that God *always* keeps His Word.

Let's remember what Jesus said. "Lazarus' sickness will not end in death. No, it happened for the glory of God, so that the Son of God will receive glory from this" (John 11:4). And even though Jesus fully understood the gravity of the situation, He waited two whole days before saying, "Let's go back to Judea." At that time, His disciples objected because of the dangerous atmosphere created by the rising animosity toward Jesus on the part of the Jewish leaders. But Jesus insisted they return to Judea. He told His disciples, "Our friend Lazarus has fallen asleep and it's time for me to wake him up."

The disciples still didn't understand—they were happy to hear that Lazarus was sleeping. They'd already "heard" that he wouldn't die, so rest, they thought, was good for those who are deathly ill. Jesus's disciples thought Lazarus must have been getting better. Imagine their surprise when they heard Jesus state plainly, "Lazarus is dead."

"What?" they might have wondered. "Didn't Jesus say Lazarus wasn't going to die?"

Did Jesus say that? No! In John 11:4, Jesus said Lazarus's sickness wouldn't *end* in death.

Sometimes, we make life harder for ourselves and we lose spiritual battles because we limit our understanding of what God can and can't do by drawing reasonable conclusions based on logical analysis. That's sensible, don't you think? In this case, Martha, Mary, and Jesus's disciples concluded that death is irreversible.

We make similar conclusions all the time! We surmise . . .

- That poor choices result in derailed lives,
- That mistakes are final,

- That broken relationships are not mendable, and

- That when Humpty Dumpty falls off the wall, the only choice we have is to clean up the terrible mess.

Am I saying that all things terrible will be reversible? No, I'm saying that for those who love God and are called according to His purpose, all things work together for good no matter how impossible they may seem at the moment. Hang in there! It's not over until God says it's over and God says in Romans 8:28 it's all gonna work out for good.

What could have seemed like a moment in time when Jesus let them down, Martha and Mary discovered that instead of letting them down, Jesus went above and beyond to do something their faith had no way of understanding was even possible. At the beginning of John 11, Martha, Mary, and Jesus's disciples knew that Jesus could prevent Lazarus from dying. By verse 41, they discovered that Jesus could raise Lazarus from the dead.

BRINGING IT ALL TOGETHER

I have always loved Martha. She's my kind of go-to woman. I can identify with what she was feeling when she got aggravated that Mary wasn't helping her get the work done. I love that between the time she sent her message to Jesus, letting him know Lazarus was sick, and the time Jesus finally showed up, *even though* her heart was broken, her brother was buried, and her prayer unanswered, Martha had already worked out her disappointment with Jesus. She wasn't going to let Romans 8:28 heckle her. Her hope was anchored in the unshakable, eternal truth of God. She understood that this life we live here on earth is not all there is for us. Even as she buried her brother, Martha was living out the hope-filled grief of a believer. She consoled herself with the solid, eternal, omnipotent goodness and love of God. And she made a powerful profession of her faith when her heart was broken.

"Martha said to Jesus, 'Lord, if only you had been here, my brother would not have died. But even now I know that God will give you whatever you ask.'

"Jesus told her, 'Your brother will rise again.'

"'Yes,' Martha said, 'he will rise when everyone else rises, at the last day.'

"Jesus told her, 'I am the resurrection and the life. Anyone who believes in me will live, even after dying. Everyone who lives in me and believes in me will never ever die. Do you believe this, Martha?'

"'Yes, Lord,' she told him, 'I have always believed you are the Messiah, the Son of God, the one who has come into the world from God.'" —John 11:21–27 (NLT)

A solid faith in God who sent Jesus to die for our

sins and who will take us to heaven when we die is good. In fact, that is the *greatest thing,* because one hundred years from now, it's the only thing that will matter to you and to me.

But on this particular day, Jesus wanted Martha to experience the supernatural evidence of a present-tense God in a present-tense world. The purpose of Jesus's timing in His response to Martha's message, the meaning to His seeming madness, was to demonstrate God's glory on earth in Bethany that day.

If you are facing a Romans 8:28 season in your life, I challenge you to entertain the possibility that God's seeming silence, His reluctance to come to your aid, His letting what is crazy go on and on and on is anchored in His plan to bring glory to God on the platform of your life.

If you are like Martha and you think your prayers were offered in vain, God is inviting you to experience the supernatural evidence of a present-tense God in your present-tense world. Every trial that invades your life brings with it a divine invitation from the heart of God to experience personally *and* to proclaim publicly the unexpected, marvelous, kingdom-building things God does. I guarantee that when you choose to seek God out even after He terribly disappoints you with His seeming absence and silence, He will always reward your devotion with greater experiences of His power and His love. When you let the glory of God flow through your life, others will really believe.

One final lesson from John 11 is this one. Because Jesus lingered and Lazarus died, many people gathered at Martha and Mary's home. Some came to grieve with them, others came to see what Jesus might do. When Jesus called Lazarus back from the dead, Scripture tells us that "many of the people who were with Mary believed in Jesus."

Don't forget that Jesus came to "seek and to save those who are lost" (Luke 19:10). If He can accomplish His goal of saving the lost on the platform of your life, then He will; for you love Him and are called according to His purpose. So the next time you find yourself in a Romans 8:28 season of life, rest in the truth of God's Word and anticipate Him working all things together for good in a way that you might have never experienced Him work before at a time when the most people will witness Him working.

PRACTICAL APPLICATION IN YOUR OWN LIFE

Remember we are "stepping out" of our pity pools. You mustered the strength to get up. And I hope you are participating in the exercises that are training your brain to fill your heart with good things so that you have a tame tongue and have learned to "shut up." And now you are ready to "step out." It's a big, scary step, and chances are, the minute you step out of your pity pool, you are going to be tempted to compare your situation to that of others and the temptation to cast blame on someone or something will wash over you like the waves that washed over Peter when he finally mustered up the courage to step out of the disciples' fishing boat that night Jesus walked on the water.

That's why I shared this chapter with you. When you are ready to step out of your pity pool, stop blaming others for the mess you're in, and take full responsibility for the life you're living, throw your anchor on Romans 8:28. For no matter what happens from this point forward, *this promise is for you*. Make it your own with this simple creative writing activity.

1. Read John 11 and take notice of the points I made in this chapter. Underline key verses and surprising interactions people had with Jesus. Note what happened before John 11 and what happened after Lazarus's resuscitation. Consider what it might have been like had you been Martha or Mary.

2. Now, think of a time in your life when something happened that caused you to question God's goodness. Pretend that you were living when Jesus lived, and you were one of his friends. Rewrite your story to reflect John 11. Include interactions you and others might have with Jesus. And consider what He might have taught people about Himself and about God in the way He responded to you. This is fiction so have fun with it.

3. Give God your story and talk to Him about His promise. Ask Him to help you hold tight to Romans 8:28 as an anchor for your faith as you venture out of your pity pool.

CHAPTER 8:

KNOW GOD IS FOR YOU

Romans 8:26–39 is custom written for us when we find ourselves in this "feeling sorry for yourself" kind of place. Romans 8:28 is so critical to having the right mindset related to the trouble you're facing that I dedicated an entire chapter to that verse. But now, it's time to take on the rest of the passage.

Here is Romans 8:26–39 in the New Living Translation.

"And the Holy Spirit helps us in our weakness. For example, we don't know what God wants us to pray for. But the Holy Spirit prays for us with groanings that cannot be expressed in words. And the Father who knows all hearts knows what the Spirit is saying, for the Spirit pleads for us believers in harmony with God's own will. And we know that God causes everything to work together for the good of those who love God and are called according to his purpose for them. For God knew his people in advance, and he chose them to become like his Son, so that his Son would be the firstborn among many brothers and sisters. And having chosen them, he called them to come to him. And having called them, he gave them right standing with himself. And having given them right standing, he gave them his glory.

"What shall we say about such wonderful things as these? If God is for us, who can ever be against us? Since he did not spare even his own Son but gave him up for us all, won't he also give us everything else? Who dare accuse us whom God has chosen for his own? No one—for God himself has given us right standing with himself. Who then will condemn us? No one—for Christ Jesus died for us and was raised to life for us, and he is sitting in the place of honor at God's right hand, pleading for us.

"Can anything ever separate us from Christ's love? Does it mean he no longer loves us if we have trouble or calamity, or are persecuted, or hungry, or destitute, or in danger, or threatened with death? As the Scriptures say, 'for your sake we are killed every day; we are being slaughtered like sheep.' No, despite all these things, overwhelming victory is ours through Christ, who loved us.

"And I am convinced that nothing can ever separate us from God's love. Neither death nor life, neither angels not demons, neither our fears for today nor our worries about tomorrow—not even the powers of hell can separate us from God's love. No power in the sky above or in the earth below—indeed, nothing in all creation will ever be able to separate us from the love of

God that is revealed in Christ Jesus our Lord."

ROMANS 8:26–30

Reread Romans 8:26–30. Underline what the Holy Spirit does for us in verse 26. How does the Holy Spirit help us pray? He prays for us! The Holy Spirit prays for us with groanings that are deeper than words. And even though you may not know exactly what is being exchanged in His groaning on your behalf, you can be confident that He is interceding on your behalf in harmony with your Father's will and in oneness with His affection for you. This is why you can be certain that God will cause everything to work together for your good.

God's own Spirit prays on your behalf. Not only does He pray, but He puts His entire heart into His prayers. He feels so deeply passionate about you that He groans with His desire for you. Some people reference this verse to support speaking in tongues as a prayer language. But I don't think praying in tongues was what Paul was talking about here. I think he was talking about the kind of communication that is far too intimate and far too important to be limited to vocabulary. It's the kind of language that was spoken between Tom and me when I grabbed hold of his hand as we walked silently to the graveside of a young father who lost his battle with cancer. It's the kind of language that I expressed when I wailed on the floor of my daughter's empty bedroom the morning after she moved out of our home. The Spirit of the living God is engaged in your life! He is so in tune with you that He groans to express His desire for you to experience the fullness of life that God is capable of giving you.

God knew you in advance. In advance of what? In advance of you knowing Him? In advance of Jesus's arrival in Bethlehem? In the beginning of time?

God knew you, and even though He knew you, and because He knew you, and even knowing you, He *chose you*. You are reading this book because *God chose you*. Of all the people in all the world, *you* are the one that He chose. God chose you and gave you the privilege of having a right relationship with Him.

According to verse 29, what is God intent on doing in you? God is intent on making you more like Jesus. Just as Kaleigh reminded us already, and reminded herself in the painful days of recent heartbreak: "God is not in the business of making us comfortable and He's not in the business of making us happy. He's in the business of making us holy."

Now I don't know about you, but I like being comfortable and I love being happy. In fact, I enjoy both comfort and happiness way more than I enjoy being squashed and crushed and chiseled upon and smashed. But there's something amazing that happens when I allow the pain of the chisel and the crushing of the anvil to have their way in me. In time (sometimes quite a long time), I discover that I understand more than I understood before. I have more compassion than I had before. And best of all, I experience the nearness of God more than I ever knew I could.

If you want to step out from your pity pool, decide this minute to be clay in the Potter's hand. Be pliable, workable, soft, and malleable.

Some time ago, I watched a potter work with her clay. She explained to us that for several minutes, she just held her hands on the clay to allow it time to "rest" in her hands. Then, she began skillfully pressing the clay with artistic precision. The clay worked with her for a bit, but then it began to resist her. She told us that when that happens, she would allow the clay to rest again, just for a bit until once again it was supple. After letting her clay rest, she began working for a second time, but the clay resisted again, and again, and finally the potter smashed her work against her potter's wheel and the clay lay like a lump. She took that lump and began working it with the same patient process she'd demonstrated before. I was hopeful that we would see an incredible vase or cup take shape at her capable hands. But the clay resisted yet again and the potter took that lump of clay and tossed it aside. She chose another lump of clay and went to work on it.

I want to be the kind of clay that learns to rest in the Potter's skilled and loving hands. I want to be the kind of clay that yields and allows Him to shape me, mold me, *and change* me into the image of Christ. I want to stop whining about the things that make me mad; I want to stop being offended by the criticism of others. I want to stop insisting the world shape to my image of what it ought to be, and instead recognize that even though I may feel my head spinning, there is a Potter who is working on me. I don't want the Potter to toss me aside because I resisted Him.

ROMANS 8:31–36

In these verses, we find some of the best questions in all of Scripture. See if you can collect them all.

1. What shall we say about such wonderful things as these?
2. If God is for us, who can ever be against us?
3. Since He did not spare even His own Son but gave Him up for us all, won't He also give us everything else?
4. Who dares accuse us whom God has chosen for His own?
5. Who then will condemn us?
6. Can anything separate us from Christ's love?
7. Does it mean He no longer loves us if we have trouble or calamity, or are persecuted or hungry or destitute or in danger or threatened with death?

What a great collection of questions! Let's answer them.
1.

1. What shall we say about such wonderful things as these?

What shall we say? The Holy Spirit helps us in our weakness. He groans forth His intercession on our behalf. And because He pleads for us in harmony with God's own heart, we can know that God causes everything to work together for our good! I say, "Amen!" "Hallelujah!" and "Praise the Lord!"

What shall you say?

2. If God is for us, who can ever be against us?

The other morning, this question bombarded my thoughts. I was minding my own business, driving toward the gym for my early morning workout (where my great trainer comes up with old lady exercises for me), and suddenly, I was pondering this thought: "Leighann, if God is for you, who can be against you?" Ponder this question with me by placing the emphasis on a different word each time you ask yourself the question:

"If *God* is for you, who can ever be against you?"

"If God is *for* you, who can ever be against you?"

"If God is for *you,* who can ever be against you?"

"If God is for you, *who* can ever be against you?"

"If God is for you, who can *ever* be against you?"

"If God is for you, who can ever be *against* you?"

"If God is for you, who can ever be against *you?*"

See how amazing that is? The God of the Universe who was and is and is to come *is for you.*

God, who is all-powerful, all-knowing, perfect in love, in wisdom, and in understanding *is for you.*

The Lord God, Maker of Heaven and Earth, the One who parted the waters of the Red Sea and fulfilled over seven hundred prophecies when He sent Jesus to be your Savior, *is for you.*

Our God, who so loved the world that He gave His only begotten Son, *is for you.*

If God is for you, who can be against you? No one. No. One.

3. Since He did not spare even His own Son but gave Him up for us all, won't He also give us everything else?

Absolutely! Of course He will! Why wouldn't He? He's already proven the extravagance of His love and the extreme measures He is willing to go to in order to call us His own. He didn't do all of this so that He could leave us destitute and lacking!

Could there be a love more extravagant than His? What else could God possibly give us to prove His love to us? What could He possibly do that would be more than He has already done?

Just camp out at the foot of the cross soaking in His amazing grace and muster up your courage to ask Him for whatever it is you need. God is eager to meet your needs according to His glorious riches. He saved you to supply you, to connect you to His wisdom and glory and honor and power.

4. Who dares accuse us whom God has chosen for His own?

   Scripture answers this question for us: "No one!" For God Himself has given us right standing with Himself.

5. Who then will condemn us?

Again, Scripture answers this question as well: "No one! For Christ Jesus died for us and was raised to life for us, and he is sitting in the place of honor at God's right hand, pleading for us" (Romans 8:34 NLT).

Let me say something about this. The picture is of a courtroom where justice is served. The interesting thing about court is that people don't always get what they are looking for when they go there. The judge and/or the jury seek to deliver righteousness. But, in court, both victims and those accused of mistreating them are represented by lawyers. Lawyers are people who've studied the law and pledged their lives to uphold it. In that sense, the lawyers, and the judge, and the jury are all on the same team. But the lawyers are hired by the victims to make sure their "rights" and their "interests" are protected according to the law. Oftentimes, those accused of wrongdoing hire lawyers to find loopholes in the law so that they will be freed from paying the consequences of their actions (if they are guilty), or they hire lawyers to gather evidence and present their side of the story so that they will be freed from paying the consequences of actions they never did (if they are innocent). Unfortunately, sometimes guilty people go free and innocent people serve time for crimes they never committed. That is a reality of the human court.

But, in the heavenlies, there is a courtroom. God sits on the Judge's seat and Jesus sits at His right hand. The Devil loves to drag you into court with trumped-up charges against you. Before you accepted Jesus's gift of salvation, He had legal jurisdiction over you. The Devil could take you or me to court and accuse us before God. He could accuse you of doing any number of wicked things. It wouldn't matter if you'd just lost your temper with your children or if you'd killed somebody. The Devil could take you before God and present his case and you would be condemned.

But the minute you invited Jesus to live and rule and reign in your life—the minute you asked His forgiveness for your sins and accepted His sacrificial death on the cross—your day in court completely changed. Now when the Devil drags you before God, he can spit and spew until his face gets red. And when he gets done, Jesus will get to have His say.

"This one's mine, Father, she's the one I love. I am for her."

And because you are His, the Father will declare, "Not guilty! You may go free."

6. Can anything separate us from Christ's love? What do you think? Can it?

7. Does it mean He no longer loves us if we have trouble or calamity, or are persecuted or hungry or destitute or in danger or threatened with death?

This is the kicker, isn't it? I mean, what put you in your pity pool in the first place? Who did you wrong? Was it trouble? Or calamity? I know someone right now who was getting his life in order. In fact, he was baptized on Sunday and then arrested on Thursday. His past caught up with him and he's struggling to fight in court even now as I write. Did these past few weeks in the county jail separate him from the love of God?

How could it? Paul, the writer of this Scripture, spent more time in jail than he did in church!

Were you persecuted? Nik Ripkin's troubling book, *The Insanity of God*, tells the stories of those who are persecuted daily for their faith. Throughout his book, he assures his readers that persecution cannot and does not separate anyone from the love of God.

Are you hungry? Destitute? In danger or threatened with death? Did someone you love die? Did they abandon you either by choice or by death? What did you lose? Did that terrible, awful thing separate you from the love of God?

When I was going through chemotherapy, I wore a little chemo pack attached to a pump. Every couple seconds, you could hear the whish of the pump pressing tiny, consistent amounts of powerfully toxic chemicals into my body. I had to wear that pump every two weeks for forty-eight hours. They told me I could die if I didn't submit myself to this treatment; the treatment itself made me feel like death might not be so bad. I was physically sicker and weaker than I had ever been in my life and I hated that pump.

My treatments came every other Monday. On the week I received chemo, I would slosh for a few days, endure the pump for a few days, and then get sick for a few days. I was never without nausea and never hungry. Nothing tasted good, and I could not touch or drink anything cold. But during the second week of recovery, I felt better and could almost pretend I felt normal again. Only Sunday night would come, and I had to face the fact that it was all going to start over again. So on most Sunday nights I cried, "I can't do this, Tom." To which he would respond, "It's hard, Leighann. But it's not too hard." And he was right, even though I felt like he was wrong. I made it, even though it was very hard.

Did suffering all of that mean that God no longer loved me? No! In fact, in suffering all of those things, I discovered depths of God's love that I never would have dug deep enough to find had I not been forced to follow Him down those dark and difficult trails.

ROMANS 8:37–39

Paul was convinced. Are you?

I found these verses poetic. I loved them! I think we sang them when I was in the Baptist Student Union Choir in college. But to live them brings an entire new level of conviction to my heart and my soul when I read them today.

I want you to understand that when you anchor your hope, your satisfaction, and your deep sense of significance in the love of God, you will step out of your pity pool and experience life like you've most likely never experienced it before.

Read verse 38 aloud. "And I am convinced that nothing can ever separate us from God's love."

Stop here. Now list all of the things that Paul listed in the "nothing" that can even attempt to separate us from God's love:

1. Death
2. Life
3. Angels
4. Demons
5. Fears for today
6. Worries for tomorrow
7. Powers of hell
8. No power in the sky above
9. No power on the earth below
10. Nothing in all creation

Now, conclude this reflection by reading the end of these verses: "Indeed, nothing in all creation will ever be able to separate us from the love of God that is revealed in Christ Jesus our Lord."

BAM!

STEP OUT!

Here is perhaps the most important thing I am going to tell you in this book. The moment you determine that God, and only God, can satisfy, strengthen, and sustain you is the minute you free yourself from any pit of any kind. Once you determine that your contentment, joy, and freedom come from what God has done for you, you will be free from the pounding waves of circumstances that you have little or no control over.

If your satisfaction is found in people, there are going to be times when people are going to disappoint you.

If your joy is anchored in life going well, there will come a day when the circumstances of life will hurt you.

If your faith is contingent on experiencing only those things that are happy and good and fun and wonderful, your faith will be shaken.

But if you focus your satisfaction on Christ alone, you will never be disappointed.

If you seek your strength from God alone, you will never be exhausted.

If you discover that the joy of the Lord will sustain you in the good times and the bad, you will overcome with overwhelming victory that is yours in Christ Jesus.

The one practical application for this chapter is this: memorize Romans 8:26–39.

CHAPTER 9:

CHOOSE TO BELIEVE

You can choose to believe what you want to believe.

You don't have to be controlled by your feelings. Feelings make great followers but very bad leaders. I love feelings! Especially the good ones. But I don't want to fall prey to the volatile unpredictability of my feelings. Anything you can take a pill to change or adjust is not worth trusting in. I am not saying that taking pills is a bad idea. I have vitamin supplements that claim to boost my mood and I enjoy taking them. I am saying that I am not going to trust what I feel as real. I'm certainly not going to trust my feelings enough to adjust my behavior around them. I am going to trust my thoughts over my feelings. And I'm going to choose to believe certain truths even when I don't feel like they are true.

You can choose to believe what you want to believe.

My granddaughter, Misty (five years old as I write this book), is my very best friend. Her little sister, River (almost two), is my very close second best friend. Misty has had a rough go of it in her five years. But she's a terrific little overcomer! Misty, like many of us, has difficulty adjusting to change. A few months ago, her other grandparents moved from the home Misty was accustomed to visiting to a new house in a community called Summertown. Misty was very concerned about this move, and had a hard time during her weekend visits while the move was going on. It was summer, and Misty loves to catch fireflies. She's quite good at catching fireflies. So in my attempt to ease Misty's concern over this change in her life, I told Misty that the fireflies were brighter in Summertown. Why wouldn't they be?

Misty believed me, simply because I told her it was true. Because Misty has a personal relationship with me, and because she's learned what to expect from me, she chose to believe me when I told her those fireflies were brighter.

You can choose to believe what you want to believe.

Because you have a personal relationship with God, and because you've walked with Him long enough to learn what you can expect from Him, choose to believe with your heart that God has given you His Word. Choose to believe that God's Word can be trusted. Choose to believe that when you're in the dark, He's still in the light; and that somehow, someway, God's going to do something wonderful for you.

"The fireflies are brighter in Summertown."

The Devil wants you to take what you've just learned in Romans 8 and convince you to interpret it to mean that if God is for you, you will live to see the circumstances of your life made into what you believe is right, fair, good, and just. The Devil guarantees you that God is obligated to exchange your heartache and trial for something incredibly wonderful. The Devil loves for you to define, predict, and lay hold of the "wonderful thing God is obligated to do for you." He especially enjoys this when you choose to define that wonderful thing with your limited understanding as you perceive life on the blip of the screen that you get to inhabit in God's great plan that spans the ages.

What is wrong with this interpretation? God did say that He would work all things together for good, which does mean the wrong in your life will be made right; and the bad in your life will be made good; and that the sorrow in your life will be turned into joy. Didn't He?

He did, so long as you trust Him to enlighten you regarding what is right, what is good, and where you find the source of true joy. Any time we try to superimpose our understanding of what is right and good and necessary for joy over what God assures us is right and good and absolutely necessary for real joy, we get snookered into believing the Devil's lies and we either wrestle with God, struggle with our faith, or turn our backs on God altogether.

GOD KNOWS WHAT IS RIGHT

Oftentimes our understanding of what is right is restricted to what is right for us. We fail to realize that when the scales tip in our favor, the people on the other side lose out. Have you ever been convinced you were right about someone, and then discovered something new and found out you were wrong? Isn't it comforting to know that God knows everything? God knows all the different angles of a situation. He knows the motives of each person involved. Not only does God know these things, but He also knows what each person did before they came to this place in their lives and what they will do in the future. God can truly size people up. He can also know when the time is right to put His plans in motion. God knows this because He knows *everything*. This alone ought to be reason enough to refuse to cast blame on others.

When you and I grow tired of waiting on God, we basically say, "I think I know better than You what should be done and I'm giving up on You." This isn't impatience; it's pride and arrogance that fails to take into account that God—and not you—knows what to do, when to do it, and how to do it best. If we could wrap our heads around the knowledge of God, we would do a whole lot more bowing down before Him and a whole lot less shaking our fists at Him.

GOD KNOWS WHAT IS GOOD

My understanding of what is good can be terribly off base. Some things I think are good turn out to be bad, and other things I think are bad turn out to be good. Last October, Kaleigh was accepted into the

International School of Medicine in Beer-Sheva, Israel. That was good. We discovered that as a student there, she'd have to learn Hebrew. That was bad. Tom and I got to visit the school in March when we took a trip to Israel and we met the administrators, toured the campus, and met a great student. That was good. Our friends then took us to see a military memorial that sat on the edge of Israel overlooking a field toward the Gaza Strip. That was bad. We heard that the terrorists who live in the Gaza Strip are intent on killing Israelis and that their missiles are aimed at Beer-Sheva. That was also bad. We heard that Israel's defense weapons have always protected their people and even when they have failed, God sent a wind to send one missile into the sea. That was good. In May, Kaleigh was accepted into medical school in Memphis, Tennessee, three hours from our home. That was *really* good.

See how our circumstances shift and change? How can we even begin to know what is and is not good? When we start thinking that we can figure this out, we can get very confused. And when our circumstances are not aligned with God's promises, we need to cling to the promise and let the circumstances happen *around* us, not *to* us. I've been stuck in a pool of pity many times because I chose to cling to my own understanding of what was and was not good instead of choosing to trust that our God who is good can deliver good in all things!

GOD GIVES JOY

How would you define joy? Is it wrapped in a package and tied with a ribbon on Christmas morning? Does joy come when two people love one another, commit their lives to one another, and invite their friends and family to share their joy? Maybe joy is delivered in a hospital and wrapped in a blanket. How would you define joy?

For many years, I thought joy was defined by my children doing what was right, and not making mistakes, and certainly not doing what was wrong in front of God and everybody else in our community. My joy was anchored in my kids being good and my family being fine and my life being "normal." But here I am several years on the other side of crazy where all the things I thought were absolutely necessary for me to know joy were removed from my life—and I've discovered there is joy in the midst of the mayhem. Had I held my breath and pitched a fit and demanded that God deliver joy on my terms, I would still be holding my breath and pitching a fit.

Instead, God delivered joy in "exceedingly, abundantly beyond what I could ever imagine" ways. He delivered joy through two beautiful little girls who call me Nana. He delivered joy by bringing all of my adult children back home to live together for a season so He could knit the heart of our family back together. God delivered joy by growing me stronger; more confident; kinder; and walking in greater peace than I've ever walked before. And He did all that when seemingly "all hell broke loose" against me.

The joy that comes from God cannot be taken away by any schemes of the enemy. The joy that comes from the Lord will strengthen and sustain you through the storm.

GOD IS FOR YOU

Aren't you ready to step out of that pity pool? Are you ready to stop blaming others? Are you ready to take responsibility for the choices you make?

God is for you!

And if God is for you, trust that He is *for* you!

No matter what is coming against you, keep your eyes focused on Him and use the "meantime" to develop the ability to trust Him when you can't imagine what He's up to.

Let me share another raw text exchange I had with my heartbroken daughter, Kaleigh, a few months ago:

Me: God knew you would need work today. He orchestrated it for you.

Kaleigh: Wish He'd orchestrate other things.

Me: He does all things well. And you can be sure He is orchestrating. Like a parent who goes Santa shopping over Thanksgiving and hides it in the neighbor's attic.

Kaleigh: But they don't give their kids the Christmas presents for a day, and then take them back.

Me: Not unless they have a very good reason that is

significant enough to risk their child's anger and severe disappointment.

I don't know if Kaleigh will appreciate my making a lesson out of her heartache. But she is so honest with God and He rewards her honesty by showing her some incredible truths. Right now, Kaleigh doesn't like what God is doing. You might not like what God is doing, and just like Kaleigh, you might not know what He's up to. But if you choose to tether yourself to His proven extravagant love for you, I promise, that in due season, you will not be disappointed (neither will Kaleigh).

I want to close this short chapter by sharing this quote with you. I saw it last weekend painted on wood in a shop called The Last Straw in Blowing Rock, North Carolina. It is said that this quote was written on the wall in a concentration camp in Germany:

"I believe in the sun even when it is not shining.

I believe in love even when I am alone.

I believe in God even when He is silent."

YOU CAN CHOOSE TO BELIEVE

What do you believe? Put your pen to paper and write a poem of your own, reflect on what we've discussed in these chapters, and write a statement of your personal belief.

Consider painting it on wood.

CHAPTER 10:

GET RID OF
SHAME AND BLAME

When my granddaughters play in my backyard, I can almost set a timer at seven minutes and know that when the buzzer goes off, they are going to ask if they can get in the pool. It's late summer here and the pool is private. I've already mentioned that Misty is five and River is about to be two. I'm telling you that so that you don't judge me when I tell you that I let Misty strip down to her undies, and River? I sometimes let River just skinny-dip. If I'm not being that lazy, I slip a swimmy diaper on her chubby little legs, and off she goes to play on the steps of our in-ground pool.

Are you judging me? I hope not!

When those two munchkins are finished in the pool, they shiver as if the temperature weren't ninety-two, and wait for me to wrap them tight with a towel. And when I wrap their squirrely little bodies tight in beach towels, they squeal with delight. Are you ready to have that much fun with your fourth step for getting out of your pity pool and back into life? Let's review how far we've come:

Step 1: Stand up—accept the realities of life and live with the limitations and possibilities those realities present.

Step 2: Shut up—stop blaming others and understand that you have the power to speak forth life into your circumstances and relationships.

Step 3: Step out—accept the fact that no matter what you are facing, God is in the midst of it. You can overcome, you can do all things, and all things will work together for good when you seek God in them.

Step 4: Dry off—if you've been splashing about in a pool of pity, chances are, you've got some leftover shame-and-blame droplets that need to be removed. In this chapter, we are going to deal with the shame first and then I'm going to show you how shame and blame make a toxic partnership.

SHAME THAT IS ROOTED IN YOUR PAST

I want you to remember a time when your feelings were hurt or you were embarrassed. I didn't even have to pause to immediately remember a comment I made to a kid when I was in the ninth grade. It was supposed to be funny, but the remark he made back to me embarrassed me and hurt my feelings. As I recall it, I feel that shame all over again! And as I was writing that sentence, I remembered something else. When I was in the tenth grade, I ran for sophomore class secretary. I made posters and taped them all over the school campus. I invited my friends to vote for me in the upcoming class elections. And then, in fifth period English class, my teacher made mention that I misspelled *secretary* on every one of those campaign posters. Much to my chagrin, I lost the election and much to hers (God rest her soul), I write books today! (Thank the Lord for spell check and editors!)

If you are like me, you don't have to think long to recall one or more situations when you were thoroughly humiliated. And the terrible thing about humiliation is the shame shadow that it leaves behind. Pity pools are shadowed by shame.

"Shame on you!"

Those three words make my skin crawl. I know that children need to be reprimanded for their wrong behavior, but to heap them with shame is . . . well, it's shameful! The goal of this chapter is to help you get rid of that shame.

SHAME IS NOT FROM GOD

Shame is not from God. I'm convinced that it's from the Devil. The Devil wants to humiliate you because humiliation cripples you with shame. So when you say the wrong thing, or do the wrong thing, or mess up royally, the Devil loves to focus your attention on the disapproval and the disappointment of others. He will even slap those scowling faces on your image of God. And where are you to go from there?

If you're not careful, you'll drag your little pity pool deep into the shadow of shame and splash about for years. The awful feeling that floods you when you mess up in front of others can be debilitating. I was talking with my sister one day about Humpty Dumpty. I've mentioned him before in this book—I'm not sure what my affection is for the ol' egghead—but on this particular day, I was explaining to Sharon that had I seen Humpty Dumpty all cracked up on the ground, I would have tried to put him back together again. Even if you told me "all the king's horses and all the king's men couldn't put Humpty together again," I would think that I could figure out a way to get the job done. I live my life by that philosophy. Sometimes it serves me well, other times it's a curse.

After I finished telling her this, my sister looked at me and said, "Leighann, this is why you and I are so very different. If I had come across Humpty Dumpty all cracked up on the ground, I would have thought, *Somehow this is all my fault.*"

I could have cried when she told me that. My incredibly talented, deeply compassionate, gifted-in-so-many-ways sister was imprisoned with shame. What she didn't know was that she was also my Humpty Dumpty and though we were sisters all my life, and I tried hard to get her not to feel that way, there never was anything I could do to free her from her prison. God miraculously freed her—it was a beautiful thing, but not the "good thing" I had imagined. She was dying of cancer when she let go of the shame that held her prisoner much of her life, and my sister lived her final days in peaceful contentment eagerly anticipating her future in heaven with Jesus.

I think I'll dedicate this chapter to Sharon. I might dedicate the entire book to her. I cannot imagine how many amazing people are stuck where they are because of the trumped-up, bogus charges that slimy "old scratch" heaves against them. (I learned last week that "old scratch" is a well-known name for the Devil that many prisoners use to refer to him.)

"Old scratch" doesn't get to do that to the children of God. Don't bow down beneath that load.

Jesus came to take your shame away. He knows you. He's seen you at your worst. He can read your thoughts and is privy to your secrets. Jesus sees you as you are and still He chooses you to have an intimate personal relationship with Him. He chooses you to be a member of His royal family. We see exactly how Jesus confronts the shame in His interaction with the woman caught in adultery. You can read her story in John 8:1–12. I've imagined what it might have been like to have been the woman and am going to share my imaginary story with you here.

THE WOMAN CAUGHT IN ADULTERY AND JESUS

She knew it was almost dawn. The birds were just beginning to sing outside her window. Oh, to have a song in her heart, and to sing boldly without a care in the world. She longed for such freedom. From the time she was very young, she knew only shame and remorse.

A long time ago, she'd known joy and true happiness. Like any other little girl, she'd gathered wildflowers and dreamt of her future husband, a happy family and children. She gently rocked her baby brother and snuggled close to his peachy soft head. She smelled his baby sweetness and wondered if she'd have a baby boy or a baby girl first.

But then her uncle came to visit. He was so fun, the twinkle in his eye and the attention he gave her drew her to him. How was she to know he had the capacity for such evil? When he came to her in the night, he placed his giant hand across her mouth and whispered harshly in her ear that if she so much as whimpered, he'd have her thrown from the cliffs into the place where all the garbage smoldered. She dare not so much as breathe as he did unspeakable things to her. When he was finished, she knew she was dirty—so dirty she'd never be clean again.

The morning after that nightmare was a blur. All she could remember was her mother's scream and her father's anger. Oh, such anger as she'd never witnessed before. Her uncle ran from her house without his robe. Her father yelled obscene things as he went.

But worse than that, her mother and father never looked at her the same again. They looked away. They were ashamed. They knew she was dirty and would never be clean again.

The sun began to peak over the corner of the night. Becca used to love this time of day, a new day with new adventures. Now she only wished for endless night, night where nothing really mattered. Darkness where she could put her body into mechanical obedience and steal perhaps a tiny morsel of some sort of wicked worth. She was reconciled to the fact that delivering physical pleasure to powerful people was the only thing she had to offer. It paid well, and she survived.

She could still smell the foul odor of onions and fish. He'd obviously enjoyed his dinner prior to his after-dinner exercise. She couldn't even remember his name—not that it mattered anyway. Suddenly, there was a noise outside her door. It sounded like men, lots of them. He cursed, pulled the covers from the pallet, and stumbled out the back. She sat up stunned as the men burst through the door and pressed in toward her. They stood staring at her as she groped for anything to cover herself. Any one of them might have sought her services in the dark of the night. But here in full day-light, they huffed and scoffed in disgust as they stared at her nakedness.

With a pompous shout, the leader of the men said,

"Woman, you will come with us! God will deal with your sin today!" Trembling, she surveyed the room. There was no escape. The men were at both doors, and they were not about to budge. She winced as two of them stepped forward and grabbed her arms in a grip that made her heart give up any hope of mercy. As the two jerked her from the pallet, yet another shoved her robe to her chest, nearly knocking her off her feet. She couldn't remember putting it on. They dragged her from her house, and she scraped her shins when she tripped over the doorframe. Bruises began to form on her arms, where their fingers dug into her flesh, and she looked at the ground.

I wonder what stoning feels like. I wonder if they'll knock me out first with a large rock to the head, and mercifully let me lay unconscious before I die. Or will they pelt me with little rocks, bruise every inch of my body, and make sport of me? I wonder if dying hurts as bad as living this shell of a life I've lived.

All these thoughts rushed through her head. Eyes— she couldn't get the eyes out of her mind. Men never looked at her with warmth. Their eyes always communicated one of two things: savage hunger or arrogant disgust. Last night and so many nights before, their eyes filled with savage hunger. Today and so many days before, it was arrogant disgust.

Suddenly, she was shoved to the ground. She dare not look up, but she felt the eyes of many looking down at her. One of the men shouted in his most pompous voice, "Teacher, this woman was caught in the act of adultery. The Law of Moses commanded us to stone such women. Now what do you say?"

Teacher, did they say *Teacher*? She'd heard of this teacher. Her cousin told her of this teacher. "You need to come meet this man they call Jesus!" she had said.

"Oh, come on. He can't be so different than all the other men!" she'd answered back.

"No, Becca (her cousin was the only person in the world who still called her by her childhood name, short for Rebecca), this man is different! Just wait until you see His eyes."

"I've seen men's eyes. They hold hunger that is easily satisfied with flesh, or they hold disgust that is only satisfied with shame. I've no need for the eyes of men," she'd responded.

"Becca, all I know is that this man is different. His eyes are full of compassion and I've only seen Him heal with His hands. Please come with me to where He's teaching today," her cousin had pleaded.

"Not today." With that, the conversation ended.

Becca couldn't resist the urge to peek at this man. Timidly, she lifted her eyes and glanced over to the one they called Teacher. He wasn't so big, and His clothes were not fancy. Unlike the men who'd paraded into her house this morning. He was surrounded by common people—men, women, and even children were sitting right up close to Him. He sat with authority and seemed to be in the middle of deep discussion when He was interrupted by their presentation. She couldn't see His face, only His body as He bent down and started drawing in the sand. What was He doing?

The man shouted out again, "What do you say, the very act! We caught her in the very act! She was still in her sin-filled bed when we found her!" Her accusers went on and on.

But He continued to draw in the sand.

Was He ignoring them? What was He doing? She had to admire the way He refused to be upset by their interruption. Finally, He stopped. He straightened up and said to them, "If any one of you is without sin, let him be the first to throw a stone at her." Then He stooped down again and continued writing in the sand.

She wondered at His answer and almost chuckled to herself at His calm response to what was obviously a trick question. Now she knew why these arrogant, religious hypocrites hated Him so. She sensed the power of His authority that would not be coerced into playing their religious games. Knowing their arrogance, she still fully expected the stoning to begin any second, so she merely smiled at His clever answer and braced herself for the first rock.

After a few seconds of silence, she noticed the oldest man sigh deeply and shuffle off away from the others. This started a quiet exit one by one of all her accusers. She watched in amazement as they walked away in silence. Before long, she was the only one still standing. She'd had her head down in shame the entire time, wishing for something in which to hide her face. Unfortunately, in their haste, the religious leaders had only grabbed her robe to cover her nakedness and hadn't even thought to provide a covering for her hair. Suddenly, she felt very much alone. She lifted her head, expecting Him to look at her with eyes filled with righteous indignation and judgment.

But as she lifted her face, she heard Him say, "Woman, where are they? Has no one condemned you?"

With the first glimpse into the perfect love of Jesus, her cousin's description came flooding back to her. She'd never seen such compassion and total acceptance as those eyes held. All her sin, all her shame, her past hurts, her wrong choices, her guilt—all of it was there, standing before this purely righteous man. And although she knew her sin was plastered all over her, somehow His eyes reflected only complete, unreserved, total acceptance and love.

Becca answered, "No one, sir."

She couldn't take her eyes from His. Before words ever formed in His mouth, she knew whatever He said, He meant. And as she marveled in His glory, she heard Him say, "Then neither do I condemn you. Go now, and sin no more."

More precious words had never been spoken.

Wouldn't it be cool to know what this woman did next? I think she found a new profession as an artistic jeweler. I like to think that she became a first-century believer and hosted prayer meetings in her home. I believe that after her encounter with Jesus, "Becca" turned her life around.

SHAME AND BLAME MUST BE SEPARATED

I asked my husband (who is also my pastor) how people overcome the Devil's shame. He said a brilliant thing (he's a brilliant man): "They embrace genuine forgiveness."

People who step out from the shadow of shame do so when they take hold of Jesus's forgiveness. The forgiveness of Christ is a marvelous gift. It's also a powerful gift! When you fully understand what it means to be forgiven, you will fully understand what life can be like without the burden of shame.

So where does blame play into all of this? It's a subtle trick, and Satan has many people snookered by it, but blame robs you of genuine forgiveness. Therefore, blame ties you to shame, and shame shuts you down.

A friend shared with me this morning the heartbreaking journey she took when her parents divorced while she was a college student. At a time in her life when holiday traditions were precious, they were stripped away and rather than get to celebrate Christmas Day with her family together, she had to divide her time between two parents. When her mother got angry at her for leaving too soon on Christmas Day, my friend had had enough. She unleashed on her mother all the pent-up frustration and anger and hurt that her parents' divorce had caused her.

My friend's relationship with her mother was understandably crippled, but after a few weeks, my friend's mother called her and began to apologize: "Honey, I'm sorry, but . . ." And she began to explain why she was justified in her position in the situation.

Have you ever been apologized to in that way?

"I'm sorry, but . . ."

How does that make you feel? It makes me feel like the person isn't really apologizing at all. They are justifying their viewpoint, and it's hard to resolve the brokenness in my relationship with them as long as they are blaming someone or something else for their behavior.

Anytime you blame someone else for your wrongdoing, you aren't taking full responsibility for your decisions. You are implying that someone or something had some kind of power over you, and that you became powerless. You are pitching the idea that they, not you, are really at fault for the predicament you are in.

When you blame others, you give up the opportunity you have to take full responsibility for your own choices. In order to experience genuine forgiveness, you have to take complete responsibility for yourself. You cannot expect to experience genuine forgiveness if your apology begins with, "I'm sorry, but . . ."

WHY BLAME IS OF THE DEVIL

Sin's nature is to shift the blame from yourself to another. When Adam ate the fruit and God confronted him with his sin, what did he do? Adam blamed Eve! When Eve was blamed for Adam's sin, what did she do? She blamed the serpent. Without anyone telling them how, both Adam and Eve naturally responded to being called out on their sin by blaming someone else.

Sin's nature is to protect "self" at all costs. To accept blame for wrongdoing could diminish power or control in a situation. When you take responsibility for yourself, you have to own it all. You have to come face-to-face with the difficult reality that you have only you to blame. Sometimes that reality is too hard to accept. The burden of shame seems easier to bear if you can drag someone under the shadow with you.

But the only way out from under the burden of shame is to take the blame—alone.

Try saying this aloud, "I am responsible for me."

Think about the people in your life. Most likely, there is one person whose love is unconditional. I hope you have a person like that in your life. I have several; my parents and my husband. Maybe my sisters, but they won't let me get away with as much as I think my parents and my husband will.

I'm a mother. There are three humans I know who can say, "There is one person who loves me unconditionally." There are two more who can say, "There is one person who loves me unconditionally and woe to the one who might dare to hurt me!" Those are my granddaughters.

Who is that person in your life? Who is the one who

loves you no matter what? It's important to know who that person is, because I'm about to tell you something about your behavior toward him or her.

Got them in mind? Print their name here:

_____

Okay, now this book just became personal and private.

Have you ever said these words to this person: "You make me so . . ."?

Have you ever said, "I wanted to . . . but you wouldn't let me"?

Anytime you use the words, "You make me . . ." or "you won't let me . . ." or any phrases like these that imply you sincerely wanted to do something different than what you did, but because of the influence of that person, you didn't do it, you are abdicating personal responsibility.

Can someone else "make" you do something against your will? Torturing and threatening the lives of those you love aside; seriously, can other people make you feel a certain way or do a certain thing or fail to do a certain thing by their behavior?

It's an honest question. You have incredible power of influence on the lives of the people you love. God created you to live interdependently with one another. You are neither dependent nor are you independent. You are interdependent. You are your best when you are living in healthy relationships with other people and those healthy relationships are created when you understand where you end and they begin.

Sin blurs those lines in relationships. Sin seeks self. When you and I seek to exalt self, protect self, satisfy self, and preserve self, we use our words and our actions to coerce, manipulate, and convince other people to adjust themselves to satisfy us. *And they do the same thing to us.* Sometimes people exploit the love of another, and use that person's feelings toward them for selfish gain. That is abuse. At other times, people with more confidence willingly take from those with less confidence and if they know they are doing this, they need to stop.

The only way to be free from this vicious cycle of people devouring people for their own personal gain is to stop living for your *self* and stop participating in the blame game. Take full responsibility for your own behavior and invite God to convince you that your self-exaltation is sin. Then confess your sin before Him, accept the forgiveness He generously gives, and "go sin no more."

THE ABC'S OF GENUINE FORGIVENESS

The practical application at the close of this chapter is this:

A—Acknowledge that you and you alone are responsible for the sin that plagues you.

Consider the memories that trigger the terrible feeling of shame. For each of those memories, ask yourself this question: Was I at fault in this situation? If the answer is yes, then accept the responsibility for your behavior and ask God to forgive you for it.

For the memories that were not your fault, make this declaration: "The Lord knows all about this situation and He knows I am not to blame. The righteous Judge declares, 'no condemnation' and therefore I refuse to accept the shame any longer."

B—Believe Romans 8:1–2 (NLT): "So now there is no condemnation for those who belong to Christ Jesus. And because you belong to him, the power of the life-giving Spirit has freed you from the power of sin that leads to death."

If you are carrying shame still from a mistake you made in your past, it's time to stop blaming yourself for that mistake. Receive the full measure of God's grace delivered through the sacrifice of His Son. Jesus paid for that mistake. He paid for that mistake in full. And Jesus knew how much suffering had to be endured to cover that. When Jesus said, "It is finished!" He declared His sacrifice completed, meaning He'd suffered enough torment for any sin you could have ever committed.

C—Confess your sin and your shame to God. Receive His forgiveness. Let the love of God wash over you again and again and again until you know beyond a shadow of a doubt that you have been forgiven.

There's a phrase from a popular chorus we sang at our church this morning. It is a fitting way to close this chapter:

"I've tasted and seen
of the sweetest of love
When my heart becomes free
and my shame is undone
Your presence Lord."[6]

Genuine forgiveness removes shame completely. Receive the forgiveness Jesus so generously offers and like the woman caught in adultery, "Go now, and sin no more."

---

6 "Holy Spirit," Jesus Culture featuring Kim Walker-Smith, Live from New York.

CHAPTER 11:

PRAISE GOD FROM WHOM ALL BLESSINGS FLOW

When my children were young, they stretched the swimming season far past late summer and into early fall. The water in the pool remained warm, but the temperature outside the pool dipped down in the evening when they hosted their pool parties. So I did what any nurturing Momma would do, and I packed the dryer full of towels and ran them on high so that when the kids got out of the pool, they not only had towels to wrap around themselves, but they had toasty warm towels to wrap around their shivering wet bodies.

Now that you've dried off the shame and blame that threaten to keep you in your pity pool, I want to encourage you to wrap yourself in the warm towel of life-giving words.

A MOUTH IN MOTION STAYS IN MOTION

Our mouths—we've dedicated an entire chapter

already to our tongues, but I want to revisit these mouths again right now. We have so much power residing in that tiny tool of a tongue. Most likely, you have been in your pity pool for quite a while, and while you've been there, you have developed the habit of talking negatively about the world around you. A mouth in motion tends to stay in motion. And if you are stuck feeling sorry for yourself, chances are, your mouth has helped to keep you there.

I have a tendency to complain. It comes very naturally to me. I don't really try to complain, it just happens. I see things that need to be fixed and I complain that they aren't fixed. When the weather's hot, I complain about the heat. When it's cold, well, I complain about that too. I have to make a concerted effort to guide my thoughts in a positive direction. But the effort is well worth it. I guide my thoughts in a positive direction by cultivating an attitude of gratitude, and by paying attention to what I'm saying. I look for funny and clever things to say rather than just spit out the first, normally negative thoughts that come to my mind.

And I'm working on not complaining. Complaining is like cluttering up your emotional and social atmosphere with debris. Complaining is to the spirit what junk food is to the body. It's really bad for you. Complaining will make you sick, and it's counterproductive. In the same way that your body craves real food even while you feed it junk, your spirit craves life-giving words even while you feed it complaints.

If you are like me and you struggle with voicing your complaints, consider this: while you can do a lot about the condition of your life, you can't control the actions, attitudes, feelings, and thoughts of others. You really can't. So don't complain when people disappoint you. Don't expect people to disappoint you but don't expect them not to disappoint you, either. In fact, most people are going to disappoint you sooner or later and there's absolutely nothing you can do to change them.

You can, however, change your response to your disappointment when it comes your way because of things you can't control. Ultimately, the only person you can control is you. And when you take full control of you, you are going to find that you don't have a whole lot of time to take care of anyone else.

You can't control whether or not some things happen to you. Your husband might be picking mangoes in the mango grove and get struck by lightning (this happened to my friend's husband). When that happens, you can complain and be angry, even bitter over your "bad luck." And if you're not careful, your bitterness will turn into an Eeyore mentality. You know Eeyore, don't you? The sad, saggy donkey in the *Winnie the Pooh* stories? If you're not careful, you will become just like him and begin to assume that terrible things are always happening to you and you will see all of life through cloudy lenses in anticipation of the next disaster.

Want to let Eeyore go back to the Hundred Acre Woods? Do what you can about the things you can control, and let go of the things you can't. Accept life for what it is: a series of good times and bad. Be vigilant in your pursuit of personal growth and development and let others be vigilant in their pursuit of theirs. If they don't seem interested in personal growth and development, don't superimpose your standards for yourself as standards for those around you. Be you, and let them be them. Accept what comes your way, and do what you can to learn from the things that are hard; celebrate with abandon those things that are easy; and be grateful that the hard times don't last forever.

We waste far too much emotional energy worrying over, complaining about, and being frustrated with things that are out of our control. Don't complain about things you can't control—just accept their reality and deal with it!

EAT FIVE SERVINGS OF VEGETABLES DAILY

I mentioned that complaining is like junk food for your spirit. Well, if complaining is like junk food for your spirit, then praise and worship is like superfood for your spirit! Don't you love the new superfoods? Like, who knew blueberries and tree nuts and all things green were so good for you? I guess Popeye knew about spinach, but his spinach came out of a can and everyone knows that the only kind of spinach that's really good for you now is the kind that is grown organically then served from farm to table in twenty-four hours. I

153

love the superfoods! I love that when I focus more on what I am eating than on what I'm not supposed to be eating, I eat more nutritiously and my body thanks me for it. So rather than "eliminate sugar from your diet," focus on eating "five servings or more of fresh fruits and vegetables daily."

You know where I'm going with this, don't you? Rather than thinking, "Don't complain, don't complain, bite your tongue, and don't say a thing," think like this, "Say at least twenty positive things to people today." Just like eating your five servings of vegetables! If I really ate my five servings of vegetables daily, I wouldn't be craving corn chips and frozen custard. Well, I might still crave the frozen custard.

It is a proven fact that you tend to see what you're looking for. You tend to see what you're focused on. If you cultivate a critical spirit, you're going to find reasons to be critical. You will be amazed at how many systems and processes could be improved upon. You will be flabbergasted over how many plans don't quite measure up; and how you'll be baffled by the many people who are less than what they should and could be. If you look for what's lacking, you will find plenty lacking. If you look for what's not right, you're going to find plenty that isn't right. If you focus on where people let you down, you're going to discover that people let you down.

But if you flip all that around and look for reasons to be supportive and encouraging, you're going to find plenty of people who will benefit from encouragement and plenty of causes and projects that are worthy of support. If you look for what is right, you're going to find plenty of things that are right. And if you look for people who are kind and compassionate, you are going to find some really amazing people. Perhaps even the things people do will begin to impress you and make you smile. Look for reasons to be supportive and encouraging, and you will find them. Not only that, but your support and encouragement will change the environment you share with them and they will begin to be different as well.

Support, kindness, and encouragement are contagious. Don't believe me? Take the challenge; intentionally support, encourage, and be kind to five people today. Track how you feel and notice how they respond. What did you discover?

ARE YOU MY CREATOR?

When my children were young, we had a little book called *Are You My Mother?* It was the story of a little duckling who was searching all over the farm for his mother. He asked the cow, the horse, the pig, and all kinds of animals if they were his mother, and although he learned all the sounds the various animals made, he didn't find his mother. Finally, the little duckling found his mother duck and knew he belonged to her because they were somewhat alike.

Many people today wander all through life looking for their Creator. We were born to worship Him, to connect with Him, and to know who we are because of the relationship we have with Him. Until we find Him, we might find many other interesting people and things to place our hope and our trust and our affection in; but we are not quite satisfied because we have not connected with the One who is like us. God knows that we need Him. He knows that we are established *in* Him. God knows that as we grow and develop in relationship with Him, we grow and develop in relationship with our self and with others. This is an aspect of *who we are* that is little understood.

Throughout Scripture, we are encouraged to spend time, emotional energy, and physical expression in praise and worship. Why? Because it's through praise and worship that we discover who our Creator is. Put yourself in that children's book. *"Are You My Creator?"* you might ask your family members. *"Are You My Purpose?"* you might ask your work. *"Do I Belong to You?"* you might ask those who are walking your journey of life with you. But when you join the angels in heaven and declare,

"Worthy is the Lamb, who was slain, to receive power and wealth and wisdom and strength and honor and glory and praise!" (Revelation 5:12 NIV)

. . . you realize to Whom you belong. And suddenly, everything in your life shifts into their proper places. Your thoughts bow down to God's perfect wisdom. You focus your affections on the things in this life that will transcend the grave. Your motivation and strength will be rooted in God; and in Him you discover that you are both unshakable and unstoppable. I am going to venture to say something profound. Are you ready? When you praise God, your whole world comes into alignment and you find your true north. *This* is why God invited us to praise Him. Not because He longs to hear our worship, but because our worship is like a cosmic magnet that draws us to the place where our world comes into order.

THANKSGIVING LEADS TO PRAISE

I just received yet another great text from Kaleigh.

"So I had the hardest emotional day I've had in a while (no idea why), so I just came home, left my phone behind, and went on a run with only the intention of running til I didn't feel like it (no goal or anything). And as I went, I just started thanking God for things like legs and oxygen and smiles and the sunset.

"On my walk back home, I ended up praying, 'I'm not asking you to change my circumstances right now. I'm asking you to change me; make me braver, more patient, better. When I'm weak, then I'm strong. The weaker I am, the stronger I am because the more I rely on you. Don't change my circumstances. Change ME. Make me better.'"

Kaleigh is going through a tough time, but instead of complaining, she began thanking God for blessings—blessings that we so often take for granted. And her thanksgiving led to praise and her praise led to surrender and her surrender led to God reaching down from heaven and giving her a *word*. Kaleigh and God have this thing for rainbows right now. She told me that when she got back to her apartment, she was scrolling through Facebook and saw not one but two pictures that friends posted of rainbows. The caption on one of them was, "Here's your sign."

Kaleigh wrote, "He's faithful. He lets it rain so that we can huddle with Him under the umbrella. He lets the battles rage so that we become stronger, braver warriors. This afternoon I felt like I was failing. And on my run, He basically said to me, 'As long as you always come back here and center on Me, it is absolutely impossible to fail.' The only thing that IS impossible with Christ is failure."

Then, she gave me this verse,

> *"In all this you greatly rejoice, though now for a little while you may have had to suffer grief in all kinds of trials. These have come to that the proven genuineness of your faith—of greater worth than gold, which perishes even though refined by fire—may result in praise, glory and honor when Jesus Christ is revealed. Though you have not seen him, you love him; and even though you do not see him now, you believe in him and are filled with an inexpressible and glorious joy."* —I Peter 1:6-8 (NIV)

When you take an honest assessment of your life, you realize that you are where you are because of the goodness of God, the gifts of others, doors opening and closing. Think not? Who fed you when you were an infant? Who changed your diapers? Who took you to the doctor when you got sick? Who taught you to read? Who took a risk on you and gave you your first job? Enough questions? No one is self-made. You are deceiving yourself if you think you are. When you put yourself on a pedestal and lay hold of the lie that you, and you alone, are worthy of honor, you not only become a person who is hard to like, but you also become a person who is seriously confused.

When you continually develop an attitude of gratitude, you take yourself off that pedestal. You stop expecting the people in your life to pay you homage and you become a likable person who is able to interact humbly in relationships and earn the respect and admiration of those around you. A gracious spirit and thankful heart is far more honest than a haughty spirit and demanding heart. When you cultivate an attitude of gratitude, you are honest with yourself and with others. You give credit where credit is due and refuse to receive any that is not due to you.

Of course we should be thankful to God. Who created gravity and atmosphere and red blood cells? Who created the sun and the moon, the tides and the seasons? To thank God for all that He's given us is to participate in the speaking forth of truth in a world where lies tend to drown out the truth. As you list your blessings and share your gratitude with others, you will begin to separate the truth from the lies. You will recognize God when He is near. You will begin to see Him working in response to your prayers. You will free yourself from the imaginary prison Satan likes to construct around believers by focusing on what he's doing. When you hang your head down and bemoan the circumstances besetting you, you are seeing only the bad stuff. When you lift up your head and give God thanks for all He has done, is doing, and is going to do, you will begin to see the good stuff.

It's time to stop talking about praise and thanksgiving and just start doing it!

PRAISE PRACTICE

Not only does the Bible encourage us to praise, but Scripture also teaches us *how* to praise. Notice, in these verses that you are given specific things you can do to praise the Lord. Consider doing one of these praise practice exercises a day for the next four days.

Day 1: Engage your body in praise.

I Chronicles 16:23–31:

23 **Sing** to the LORD, all the earth; **proclaim** his salvation day after day.

24 **Declare** his glory among the nations, his marvelous deeds among all peoples.

25 For great is the LORD and most worthy of praise; he is to be feared above all gods.

26 For all the gods of the nations are idols, but the LORD made the heavens.

27 Splendor and majesty are before him; strength and joy are in his dwelling place.

28 **Ascribe** to the LORD, all you families of nations, **ascribe** to the LORD glory and strength.

29 **Ascribe** to the LORD the glory due his name; **bring an offering and come before him. Worship** the LORD in the splendor of his holiness.

30 **Tremble** before him, all the earth! The world is firmly established; it cannot be moved.

31 Let the heavens **rejoice**, let the earth **be glad**; let them say among the nations, "The LORD reigns!"

Make a list of the words in **bold** type. Do you know what each of those means? I wasn't sure about *ascribe* so I looked it up for you: *Ascribe* means "to credit someone with the honor due them for something they have done or some characteristic they demonstrate." When you "**ascribe** to the LORD the glory due his name," you acknowledge that God is worthy of credit for all that He is and all that He has done.

Praise involves action. Try participating in some of these specific actions for the next five minutes: sing, proclaim, declare, ascribe, tremble, rejoice, and be glad.

Day 2: Praise focuses attention on the characteristics and attributes of God.

Psalm 99:

1 The LORD **reigns,** let the nations tremble; he sits enthroned between the cherubim, let the earth shake.

2 **Great** is the LORD in Zion; he is **exalted over all the nations.**

3 Let them praise your **great and awesome name—** he is holy.

4 The **King is mighty, he loves justice**—you have established equity; in Jacob you have done what is just and right.

5 Exalt the LORD our God and worship at his footstool; **he is holy.**

6 Moses and Aaron were among his priests, Samuel was among those who called on his name; **they called on the LORD and he answered them.**

7 **He spoke to them** from the pillar of cloud; they kept his statutes and the decrees he gave them.

8 LORD our God, **you answered them;** you were to Israel a **forgiving God,** though you punished their misdeeds.

9 Exalt the LORD our God and worship at his holy mountain, for the LORD **our God is holy.**

Notice in Psalm 99 the various characteristics or attributes of God that are worthy of praise. Make a list of the words in **bold** type.

Day 3: Praise attunes your ears to the voice of God.

Psalm 29:

1 Ascribe to the LORD, you heavenly beings, ascribe to the LORD glory and strength.

2 Ascribe to the LORD the glory due his name; worship the LORD in the splendor of his holiness.

3 The thunders voice of the LORD is over the waters; the God of glory, the LORD thunders over the mighty waters.

4 The voice of the LORD is powerful; the voice of the LORD is majestic.

5 The voice of the LORD breaks the cedars; the LORD breaks in pieces the cedars of Lebanon.

6 He makes Lebanon leap like a calf, Sirion like a young wild ox.

7 The voice of the LORD strikes with flashes of lightning.

8 The voice of the LORD shakes the desert; the LORD shakes the Desert of Kadesh.

9 The voice of the LORD twists the oaks and strips the forests bare. And in his temple all cry, "Glory!"

10 The LORD sits enthroned over the flood; the LORD is enthroned as King forever.

11 The LORD gives strength to his people; the LORD blesses his people with peace.

In Psalm 29, we get a glimpse of the heavenlies and learn the power of the voice of the Lord. Make a list of all the things that happen when the Lord speaks.

What does God do for His people? What does He do when we praise Him? Remember this!

Day 4: Praise draws you to the throne of God.

Revelation 4:8–11:

8 Each of the four living creatures had six wings and was covered with eyes all around, even under its wings. Day and night they never stop saying: "Holy, holy, holy is the Lord God Almighty," who was, and is, and is to come.

9 Whenever the living creatures give glory, honor and thanks to him who sits on the throne and who lives for ever and ever,

10 the twenty-four elders fall down before him who sits on the throne and worship him who lives for ever and ever. They lay their crowns before the throne and say:

11 "You are worthy, our Lord and God, to receive glory and honor and power, for you created all things, and by your will they were created and have their being."

This is a rare preview of what we are going to see when we get to heaven. Just as a review, there were four _____ with six _____.

When they worship the Lord, twenty-four _____ fall down, lay their crowns before the throne, and say, "You are worthy . . ."

Pretend you are one of those twenty-four elders. You are standing before the throne of God. Fall down before Him, lay down your crown, and proclaim with the elders, "You are worthy, our Lord and God, to receive glory and honor and power, for you created all things, and by your will they were created and have their being."

CHAPTER 12:

TURN YOUR SETBACKS INTO SETUPS FOR GOD TO SET THINGS STRAIGHT

Which one among us has lived a life with no regrets? When my firstborn was a week old, I remember sitting at the table in the kitchen and telling my mother how determined I was to do things right. I said, "I want her to get on the school bus in a few years and know, beyond a shadow of a doubt, that I have lived my life as her mother with no regrets."

My sweet momma smiled knowingly and said, "That would be great."

To live your life with no regrets is ambitious. My firstborn is twenty-four and believe you me, I've got a ton of regrets! I had plenty the first year of her life and lost count of them by her second birthday. Most of us will let people down. Most of us will let ourselves down. Most of us will let others down. And most of us will, at some time, be plagued with "shoulda, woulda, coulda" regrets. It's normal.

J. K. Rowling said, "It is impossible to live without failing at something, unless you live so cautiously that you might as well not have lived at all—in which case, you fail by default."

We all fail, we all have regrets, and we all fall down, experience setbacks, endure bad luck, and are recipients of the wrong done to us. All of this is normal. But just because you experience what everyone else experiences doesn't mean you have to respond to those experiences like everyone responds. In fact, the difference between the successful few and the ordinary masses is not rooted in chance, or an abundance of golden opportunity. The difference between those who succeed and those who don't is found in what those who succeed do with failure or setbacks.

Consider these famous successful people:

1. **Oprah Winfrey.** Oprah was fired from her first television anchor position in Baltimore. Today, she is a billionaire who owns her own television network. In a speech at Harvard, Oprah said this about failure: "There is no such thing as failure. Failure is just life trying to move us in another direction."

2. **Steven Spielberg.** Did you know that Steven Spielberg was rejected twice by the University of Southern California's Cinematic Arts? A few years ago, the university built a building in his honor.

3. **Walt Disney.** Walt had a newspaper editor who told him that he "lacked imagination and had no good ideas." Disney said this about failure: "I think it's important to have a good hard failure when you're young . . . Because it makes you kind of aware of what can happen to you. Because of it, I've never had any fear in my whole life when we've been near collapse and all of that. I've never been afraid."

4. **Dr. Suess.** Dr. Suess's books were rejected by twenty-seven different publishers. They eventually went on to sell over 600 million copies worldwide (and I can't imagine the royalties on all the quotes that can be found on T-shirts, ball caps, framed art, and other forms of expression today). [7]

Just by reading this book, you have chosen not to be normal anymore. You've decided to look at your own failures, regrets, and setbacks from another angle. While most people blame others, you are taking responsibility for the choices you make. You are holding the reins of your life and learning to ride with grace and poise. So, when you do things you wish you hadn't, or don't do things you wish you had, you get to maneuver those

---

[7] Kipman, Sebastion. "15 Highly Successful People Who Failed on Their Way to Success." http://www.lifehack.org/articles/productivity/15-highly-success-ful-people-who-failed-their-way-success.html.

setbacks into a place where God can step in and do far more than you could have ever imagined possible.

This chapter is about turning your setbacks into set-ups for God to set things straight. Just think how much more pleasant your outlook on life would be if you could take your setbacks and see them as seeds planted in the ground of experience certain to yield a robust harvest in due season. And what if I told you, that is exactly what they are.

GOD SET THINGS STRAIGHT IN SCRIPTURE

Oh, did He ever! God will set things straight as often as you yield yourself to Him and allow Him to be involved in the details of your life. One of my key life verses is:

"The Lord directs the steps of the godly. He delights in every detail of their lives." —Psalm 37:23 NLT

The Lord not only directs my steps, but He also delights in paying close attention to the details of my life. Translated, this means that God, the Lord of the Universe who created all that exists, takes special interest in directing my path and working with the details of my life. He doesn't miss one tear; He doesn't look over one desire; the God who knows the number of hairs on your head *delights in every detail of your life.* That is a powerful thought. Ponder it for a minute.

Now, I want to take you on a journey through the

life of Joseph. Before you go with me, read Joseph's story in your Bible. And as you read, ask yourself these questions:

- How did his brothers' jealousy impact Joseph's thoughts about himself?
- How did his brothers' behavior impact Joseph's thoughts about God?
- How did the setbacks in Joseph's life set him up for God to set things straight?

Joseph's ordeal is one of many stories in Scripture where God intervened in a person's life in order to advance His cause. As you consider your own life in the story of Joseph, be sure to remember that God has a great plan and that His plan will not be thwarted (Job 42:2). God invites you to join Him in His plan. If you choose to RSVP to God's invitation and commit your life to the building and advance of God's kingdom, then you can be sure that God will direct your steps just as He directed Joseph's steps. You can also be certain that God will delight in even the tiniest details of your life, just as He delighted in the details of Joseph's life. Before you read my retelling of Joseph's story (with running commentary), read the story for yourself in your favorite translation of Scripture. Joseph's story is found in Genesis 37 and 39–47. I'm reading the New Living Translation as I reflect on this fascinating account of one man's life.

JOSEPH BEFORE THE PIT

Joseph's story began when he was seventeen years old and working for his half-brothers. They were most likely several years older than Joseph, and they were doing "bad things." Joseph told his father about the bad things his brothers were doing. It is just after hearing that Joseph was a tattletale that we also get a greater understanding of Joseph's greatest issue in life. In Genesis 37:3–4, we find out that Joseph was his father's favorite and that he'd been born to Jacob in his old age. Jacob made no excuse for his favoritism and lavished Joseph with his affection, specifically in the form of a beautiful robe. Joseph's brothers hated Joseph and his robe, and "they couldn't say a kind word to him."

Have you ever been despised because someone else favored you? Has anyone ever been jealous of you? How did it feel to be the recipient of their disdain and be powerless to change their mind or their actions toward you? I'm not sure she was jealous of me, but I do know what it's like not to be liked by someone, and to have unkind things said about me. It's hard—especially in our current culture of social media! I want to say things I should not say when Facebook asks, "What's on your mind?"

Joseph didn't have Facebook, but he did have dreams. And with no regard for a filter, he proclaimed his dreams to his brothers. He might have enjoyed telling them that he'd been given a glimpse of them someday bowing down before him. But his telling his jealous brothers those dreams didn't do him any good in helping them all get along better.

When Jacob asked Joseph to go on a journey to check on his brothers, he was asking Joseph to take a big trip. The distance between Hebron and Shechem is over eighty-eight miles. That was quite the journey. When Joseph arrived in Shechem and couldn't find his brothers, he might have asked God to help him. I would've prayed about it if I were him. After traveling that many miles, I'd hate to have to go home without a report. We don't know if Joseph prayed or not, but a man told him that his brothers were headed toward Dothan. Dothan was thirteen more miles past Shechem. How many miles can a man walk in a day? Fifteen? Twenty? It took a lot of time for Joseph to find his brothers.

But when his brothers saw him coming, they schemed to kill him. Wow. They'd been gone for months, Joseph had walked for at least a week to catch up with them, and their first thought was to kill him. Goodness. Brother Reuben convinced his brothers not to kill him, but to let nature do the dastardly deed. He suggested tossing Joseph into an empty cistern and just leaving him there until he died.

I can't think of a worse way to go. Well, maybe I can. But being tossed in a cistern and left to die would be tremendously lonely.

But then we read that Reuben never intended to

leave his little brother in that cistern but planned to rescue him and return him to his father. Way to go, Reuben! Only, things didn't work out the way Reuben hoped they would.

When Joseph reached his destination, his brothers stripped him of his robe and tossed him in the cistern. Then, they sat down to eat. Can you imagine how lonely Joseph must have been to have all those brothers all his life, and no camaraderie with them? To always be on the outside looking in, never at the campfire with them, never sharing stories and jokes and silent expressions that spoke volumes without speaking? Do you know anyone who has lots of people around them but suffers severe loneliness? Don't assume that just because people are the center of attention they get enough attention. Often the loneliest person in the room is the loudest one.

But just as the brothers were getting ready to eat, they saw a caravan of Ishmaelite traders headed to Egypt. Brother Judah had the brilliant idea to sell Joseph to the Ishmaelite traders. Brother Judah had some questionable morals. You can read more of his interesting story in Genesis 38. But back to Joseph. His brothers decided Judah's idea was a good one so they pulled Joseph out of the pit and sold him to the Ishmaelite traders for twenty pieces of silver. (Jesus was sold by Judas for thirty silver pieces way later in Scripture.)

I don't know where Reuben was when his brothers sold Joseph to the Ishmaelites, but he came back later and discovered Joseph missing. After the fact, Reuben made an interesting decision to go along with his brothers and betray his father by lying to Jacob to cover up their shameful deed. Jacob was devastated when Joseph's brothers returned with his beautiful robe drenched in blood, and he "mourned deeply for his son for a long time." I wonder how Reuben, Judah, and all the other boys slept at night when they heard their father weeping.

Let's stop right here and take an account of Joseph's setbacks in life. At seventeen years old, his brothers despised him and were cruel to him. At about that same age, he was sold *by his own brothers* into slavery and ended up in Egypt, far from his home and from the only people who loved him. You wouldn't expect a boy like this to become a great leader. You'd expect him to end up in prison someday (which he did, but not because of his own wrongdoing).

JOSEPH AFTER THE PIT

Joseph's story continues in Genesis 39 with a quick recap and then this interesting statement, "The LORD was with Joseph, so he succeeded in everything he did as he served in the home of his Egyptian master." Remember my verse, Psalm 37:23? Did the Lord direct Joseph's steps? In reading his story, it certainly seems like Joseph's brothers, jealousy, and greed directed Joseph's steps. But according to Psalm 37:23, the Lord directs the steps of the godly. A subtle lie we inadvertently embrace is, "If God is directing my steps, I can expect to find myself in pleasant places."

I wish that were so. And sometimes, wise choices and God's grace do carry us through fertile valleys and beside still waters where our cups overflow. But sometimes, God's plans carry the godly into dark cisterns and foreign lands. God's plans might carry God's committed servants into prison. That's exactly where God's plan carried Joseph. Because Joseph was a godly man, he was falsely accused of a crime he did not commit and the man who once entrusted him with everything tossed him into prison. Joseph would have never ended up in prison in Egypt had he not experienced the setback of being sold into slavery by his brothers and then falsely accused of making advances toward Potiphar's wife.

But, once Joseph went from the palace to the prison, we again read this, "But the LORD was with Joseph in the prison and showed him his faithful love. And the LORD made Joseph a favorite with the prison warden." Before long, the warden put Joseph in charge of everything.

Let's stop again and make some observations. We can add to Joseph's list of setbacks: being sold to Potiphar and then falsely accused of attempted rape with Potiphar's wife because Joseph refused to sleep with her. This false accusation from Potiphar's wife led to Joseph being tossed into prison. All along, Joseph was simply doing what he was told to do. Nowhere along the way did Joseph get what was coming to him or reap the rewards of his good decisions in life. The seeds Joseph had sown did not produce the harvest he was suffering. Have you ever been there? Joseph could have easily cried, "This isn't fair!"

But he didn't. Instead, Joseph served God in the right now. At Potiphar's house, Joseph learned how to run an Egyptian household and to manage Egyptian property. He became an administrator and the work he did prospered. When Joseph found himself in prison, God ministered to him there. The Scripture specifically says that God was "with" Joseph and that He "showed him his faithful love." God might direct your steps to a dark place, but He promises to be with you there and to show you His faithful love *in that place*. It was in prison that Joseph felt the love of his heavenly Father and learned how to manage people. The prison warden put Joseph in charge of all the other prisoners; what a great way to learn the art of leading people!

So, while Joseph was suffering one setback after another, he was training to become a manager of Egypt's wealth, an administrator of Egypt's resources, and a leader of Egypt's people. He didn't get to attend the University of Cairo and major in business administration with a concentration in leadership development, but God created a customized educational/career track, and Joseph followed it. Chances are that if you are in a place where you have suffered one setback after another, you might also be enrolled in one of God's personal development plans.

JOSEPH SET STRAIGHT

Joseph spent many years of his life suffering the effects of the sin and misbehavior of others. He landed in a cistern because of jealousy; he landed in Potiphar's house because of greed; and he landed in prison because of lust. But eventually, God put Joseph in charge of the whole land of Egypt and second in position with only Pharaoh ranking higher than him. Only God could do such a thing. And God knew all along where Joseph was headed. He even gave Joseph some dreams to hang on to in the meantime. Joseph might have been heckled by those dreams at times. But in due season, Joseph's dreams proved to be true, God's plans were accomplished (they always are), and Joseph's brothers were humbled.

You know the rest of the story so I'm not going to take time to tell it. If you don't know the rest of the story, please do take time to read it. You will be so glad you did. You can find the rest of the story in Genesis 27–42. What I want you to know right now is that Joseph's responses to his setbacks were critical in his well-being along the way; in his learning what he needed to know for the future; and in his being prepared for God's setting things straight.

LESSONS TO LEARN FROM JOSEPH

1. Trust God and live in the present.

Joseph could have lived in the past and grieved

himself to death over his separation from his parents and his little brother. When Joseph's brothers came to Egypt, Joseph's reaction revealed his deep affection for his family. He could have easily allowed his brothers' treachery to ruin his life. Joseph also could have sat in prison nursing his bitterness over doing the right thing and then being punished for doing what was wrong. He could have shut himself off from all the others and spent days, months, even years nursing a grudge. What good would that have done him?

Instead, Joseph trusted God and lived in the present. When Joseph was with Potiphar, he served Potiphar well. When Joseph was in prison, he served the prison warden well. When Joseph was second in command in Egypt, he served the Egyptians well. It wasn't until Joseph was reunited with his brothers that he understood the extent to the famine and saw the hand of God in his life.

When your life is riddled with setbacks, trust God and live in the present.

2. Trust God and do good.

Joseph chose to not only live in the present but to also do good. Everywhere Joseph went, he left that place better than he found it. What a great way to live! I am certain that Joseph slept a bit better in the dungeon because he knew he'd encouraged the prisoners, settled disputes, improved conditions, and enhanced the quality of life for those in jail. No matter where you are, you can find ways to do good. I love the stories of those who suffer tragedy and rather than wrap themselves in a blanket of desperation, they reach out and offer encouragement to others who are suffering their own tragedies as well. If you take a look around you, you will find that you can do good no matter where you are.

3. Trust God and explain Him to others.

Joseph put the pieces of his life together and saw God's big picture. He knew that God had directed his steps and delighted in the details of his life. And because Joseph chose to go with God, he didn't let bitterness or animosity cloud his thinking. When he was reunited with his brothers, Joseph explained God's plan to them.

If you go with God and trust Him to direct your steps, the pieces will eventually fall into place. When they do, take the time to explain God's methods to others.

GOD IS SETTING THINGS STRAIGHT TODAY

Somewhere along the way, Joseph had to let go of the way he might have thought his life was supposed to be and instead accept it as it was. Life does that to us. Cancer gave me a gift. It gave me several gifts, really, but one of them was this: no matter what today brings, it's still a gift to get to live it. None of us are guaranteed tomorrow, and the only life we ever live is the life we're living right now. Stop being angry over what hasn't happened for you; stop being angry over what has happened to you; and simply live today in the quiet and peaceful assurance that God is near and His faithfulness endures forever.

I love this quote by Marc and Angel Hack (popular authors of an online personal development blog): "The richest person isn't the one who has the most but the one who needs the least." It reminds me of Paul's quote in Philippians 4:11–13 (NIV):

"I am not saying this because I am in need, for I have learned to be content whatever the circumstances. 12 I know what it is to be in need, and I know what it is to have plenty. I have learned the secret of being content in any and every situation, whether well fed or hungry, whether living in plenty or in want. 13 I can do all this through him who gives me strength."

When you truly believe that the Lord directs the steps of the godly and delights in the details of your life, you will be content in whatever circumstances you find yourself in. You will not need more because you have enough. Sometimes it is in the most desperate times that we realize Jesus is quite enough.

If Joseph were sitting with us today, He would most likely say, "Happiness, my friends, is not the absence of problems but rather the ability to properly deal with them." Trouble, Jesus said, is guaranteed. Peace is optional (see John 16:33). If you choose to go with Jesus, He will give you His peace. But going with Jesus requires letting go of the right to live a life of earthly prosperity, situational happiness, and ease. Going with

Jesus requires letting Him and Him alone determine the next step for you.

I read an amazing article this morning. Kaleigh texted me the link. It's a 500-word essay written by a musician and sound engineer who suffered a terrible tragedy on April 27, 2016. David Platillero eloquently explains how his faith allowed him to discover the true reality of redemption because of his accident. "Suffering is an opportunity to find new meaning. I have a hope that the meaning of all this suffering is to gain a platform from which to proclaim the God who takes broken situations and redeems them for His glory and our good!" David nailed it.[8]

God is always in the business of setting things straight. You will begin to see Him at work when you choose to trust Him.

TURN YOUR SETBACKS INTO SETUPS FOR GOD TO SET THINGS STRAIGHT

1. Just as you did with Joseph, review the story of your own life. Make a list of your setbacks. For each one, respond to these questions:

   • How did you feel when this happened to you?
   • What did you learn from this experience?

---

8 Please take time to read David's article here, http://www.knoxnews.com/entertainment/life/personal-faith-accident-changes-belief-about-pain-3ac0aa40-9be0-3f2d-e053-0100007f261b-392174431.html.

- How did you respond?
- How do you wish you'd responded?

2. Now consider each one of those situations. How might you follow Joseph's example and trust God with each one? Carefully answer this question by considering these things:

- If that setback resulted in some kind of loss, what did that loss create opportunity to gain? For instance, if you lost a friendship, how could you invest the emotional energy and physical time you used to put into that friendship into something or someone else?
- If that setback put you somewhere you wouldn't have been otherwise, what good can you do in that place? For instance, if you were diagnosed with cancer, how might you minister to others in the oncologist's office?

3. What would it look like for God to set this thing straight?

- Invite God to give you imagination and see outside the box created by your preconceived notions.
- Thank God for the possibilities and invite Him to do exceedingly abundantly more than you could ask or imagine.

4. Pray: *Father, I want to be a godly woman. Please direct my steps. And if the direction you*

take me is through difficult places, remind me You are near. Father, I invite You to delight in the details of my life. I trust Your delight and long to know You more. I trust You and I want to do good. Amen.

CHAPTER 13:

LIVE YOUR LIFE WITHIN GOD'S BOUNDARIES FOR YOU

This book is coming to a close, and in this, our final chapter, I'm going to put a great big "!" on the entire message by talking about boundaries. And since I need this chapter as much, if not more, than any of my readers, I'm going to share with you what I have learned in researching this powerful, life-altering subject.

When I was a little girl, my parents maintained boundaries for me. They decided what I would eat for breakfast and when I would go to bed at night, and they determined most everything that happened in between. But as I grew older, I gained more freedom and began to determine boundaries for myself. Once I had my driver's license, I decided how fast I would drive and what time I headed home. My parents helped me make wise decisions of my own by implementing curfews and consequences when I chose not to live inside what they considered smart boundaries. The boundaries my parents established were to teach me how to eventually live responsibly on my own. Their boundaries were lovingly established to protect me and to empower me.

But I didn't see boundaries like that. Somewhere along the way, I decided that boundaries were restricting. I wanted to resist them, to press against them, and to see what was on the other side of them. I bought in to the lie that boundaries were bad rather than good. I didn't rebel so much as I just wanted to prove the tried-and-true principles of life wrong. Just because other people couldn't do it all didn't mean I couldn't; or so I thought. Remember Humpty Dumpty? All the king's horses and all the king's men had limits to what they could and couldn't do, not me. It wasn't until I began studying this concept of boundaries that I realized I wasn't being driven by mysterious superpowers. I was struggling with establishing personal boundaries and being confident that they were good, not bad. I didn't know when to say yes and when to say no because the borders between others and me were blurred. My own insecurities played into this.

Life would be chaotic and scary without boundaries. The "limits" or the "lines" define the "game." Without them, we wouldn't know how to define success. We wouldn't know how to define our lives' purposes or our goals. People who set and keep boundaries are people who know why they are here and what they want to accomplish. They understand who God says they are and what His purpose is for them being here. They are committed to fulfilling their life's goals and they resist the pressure that comes when other people overstep the imaginary lines that define them and impose *their* values and goals on them.

Do you live with well-defined boundaries? Do you know where you begin and where you end? Do you know what you want to accomplish in life and therefore how to clear the clutter so that you can accomplish those things? If not, you are going to be glad that you picked up this book and made it to this chapter. Keep reading. You are going to be set free to live your life without blaming others, taking full responsibility for the choices *you* make and being confident that those choices are the best ones for you.

WHAT ARE BOUNDARIES?

In order to figure this all out, we need to define what we mean when we talk about boundaries. The best definition I know comes from the boundaries guru Dr. Henry Cloud. He, along with Dr. John Townsend, wrote much on the subject. Here is Dr. Cloud's definition:

"Boundaries, in a broad sense, are lines or things that mark a limit, bound, or border. In a psychological sense, boundaries are the realization of our own person apart from others. This sense of separateness forms the basis of personal identity. It says what we are and what we are not, what we will choose and what we will not choose, what we will endure and what we will not, what we feel and what we will not feel, what we like and what we do not like, and what we want and what we do not want. Boundaries, in short, define us. In the same way that a physical boundary defines where a property line begins and ends, a psychological and spiritual boundary defines who we are and who we are not." [9]

Dr. Cloud goes on to say that there are nine things that define you as a person: your physical appearance, your attitudes, your feelings, behavior, thoughts, abilities, desires, choices, and limits.[10] He says that these are the things you and I are personally responsible for. These nine things belong inside your property lines. You and you alone are responsible for your appearance, attitudes, feelings, behavior, thoughts, abilities, desires, choices, and limits. To give responsibility to others in these areas of your life is to render yourself powerless.

Think on these things.

Now let me quote Barrie Davenport who has a great article on boundaries online:

"There is one area of personal evolution that can make or break your self-esteem and your ability to have healthy relationships. It's the ability to set and implement healthy personal boundaries. Personal boundaries are the imaginary lines we draw around ourselves to maintain balance and protect our bodies, minds, emotions, and time from the behavior or demands of others. They

---

9   Dr. Henry Cloud, "Changes that Heal; The Four Shifts that Make Every
    thing Better...And That Anyone Can Do," Zondervan, 1992, p. 92.
10 IBID, pp. 96–110.

provide the framework to keep us from being used or manipulated by others, and they allow us to confidently express who we are and what we want in life. Personal boundaries allow us to be in the driver's seat of our own lives. Without healthy boundaries or with very weak boundaries, you simply **cannot have healthy relationships.** You give up a part of yourself to be available or accommodating. Or you become so entangled with another person and their needs (co-dependent behavior) that you lose your own identity. This undermines your integrity and leads to a loss of self-respect—and the respect of those around you."[11]

If you're like me, just reading that quote causes you to have uncomfortable feelings of anger, frustration, guilt, and resentment. The lack of healthy boundaries is what is at the root of your tendency to blame others for all that's not right in your world. If you can blame them for what you feel, how you're behaving, or the frustration you've decided to endure, then surely it's their fault and not yours, right?

Wrong.

When you blame others for things that are your responsibility to control, you are still at fault; and your main problem is a breach of your boundaries. Your "fences" are broken. When your boundaries are not well-defined, you allow others to disrupt your life with their agendas for you.

---

11 Barrie Davenport, "Ten Ways to Establish Personal Boundaries." http://liveboldandbloom.com/08/life-coaching/want-to-boost-your-self-esteem-10-ways-to-establish-personal-boundaries.

Mark Manson said this (and I love it):

Healthy Personal Boundaries = Taking responsibility for your own actions and emotions, while NOT taking responsibility for the actions or emotions of others.[12]

Boundaries serve two purposes: to keep intact those parts of you that make you *you*; and to resist the pressure that loved ones might exert on you to take on the parts of them that they might want to place on you. Just like good fences make good neighbors, so do good boundaries make healthy family relationships, marriages, and friendships.

HOW TO DEVELOP HEALTHY BOUNDARIES

So how do you develop healthy boundaries? I'm glad you asked. Here are four ways you can develop healthy personal boundaries.

1. Know that boundaries are both necessary and good.

Borrow my life sentence, "I am a person of worth, created in the image of God to relate and to live." (This is a sentence I discovered in the seventh grade. It's written by Grady Nutt, and I adopted it to be my life sentence.) Borrow that sentence and add a bit to it. Say this aloud, "I am a person of worth created in the image

12 Mark Manson, "The Guide to Strong Boundaries." https://markmanson.net/boundaries.

of God to relate and to live. My life is a gift and I get to choose how to live it."

Thank God that you get to choose! God gave you free will when He created you as an individual. You, not your mom, not your dad, your sister or brother, spouse, best friend, or kids. *You* choose who *you* want to be.

You came into this life at a moment in time and took your first breath. You will leave this life in a moment of time and breathe your last. You, and only you, get to determine what you will do in between your first and your last breath. What you do with the dash between the lines is up to you. In order to protect yourself from the people who want you to take responsibility for their dashes and in order to guard your dash from them, you need to understand and accept that boundaries are both necessary and good. And you get to create your own boundaries!

2. Understand what it means to be "a part of" someone and what it means to be "apart from" someone.

Dr. Cloud describes the first year of life as a year of "bonding." Although a newborn baby is separate from his mother's body, he is connected to his parents and other caring adults during the first year of his life. As a baby grows, he develops security and safety in belonging to his family. This year of bonding gives that baby what he needs in order to grow to understand his sepa-rate-ness or individuality.

As the baby grows, he begins to differentiate himself from others. He starts walking, falls down, and realizes that his own walking led to his falling. My granddaughter has just graduated to the freedom of a toddler bed. She and her mother are adjusting to her discovery of her separate-ness at bedtime!

As life goes on, a preschooler, then school-aged child finds out that he gets to choose his own behavior. With good parenting, he will suffer the consequences of bad choices. In order to be good parents, we must not only allow our children to suffer the consequences of their poor choices but also see to it that some of their wishes are not granted. It's only in dealing with disappointment that our children learn to own their own thoughts and actions. (I wish I had known this when my own children were preschoolers!)

Dr. Cloud said this about the developing child: "If he is allowed to have his thoughts and wishes without having all of them gratified, he learns how to own what he thinks, feels, and chooses, without being out of control. This is the delicate balance of being allowed to 'be all of who his is' and not being able to be 'all there is.' This is the balance of being able to have a self without being self-centered."[13]

Dr. Cloud goes on to explain that ownership is absolutely essential in creating boundaries. For those people who are not allowed to own their feelings, behavior, desires, thoughts, and choices, they fail to develop a

---

13 Cloud, <u>Changes that Heal,</u> p. 115.

real sense of responsibility. They refuse to take responsibility for themselves, because they are accustomed to other people either paying the consequences of their decisions or taking responsibility for them. Then, on the flip side, there are other people who take responsibility for the choices, feelings, behavior, thoughts, and desires of others. For those people, they take away ownership from another and end up destroying the very relationships they are trying so desperately to maintain.

Now, let's get personal. Consider the people most precious to you. Are these the people you "belong" to? Are they your family members or friends? If so, how are you like them and how are you different? In what ways do you become a part of them? In what ways do you maintain your individuality?

Have you ever accused this person or these people of taking one of your nine "things" from you? (Remember the nine things: your appearance, attitudes, feelings, behavior, thoughts, abilities, desires, choices, and limits.) In what ways have you relinquished ownership of these things to these people? In what ways have they attempted to take these things from you?

When my daughter Kaleigh was in the eighth grade, she had a hard time deciding whether or not she wanted to continue playing softball on the middle school team. We enjoyed watching her and her sister play ball together for years. Kaleigh was a good ball player, and she was very tall. This made her a great first baseman. Her dad especially enjoyed watching his kids play ball, and when Kaleigh started hinting at the possibility that she might not play, Tom began to encourage her not to quit. Kaleigh weighed her options and continued to lean on the side of giving up softball as an extracurricular activity. But to please her dad, Kaleigh practiced with the team. On the first day of practice, she heard the coach's brother curse and saw him chewing tobacco. Kaleigh has always been a stickler for the rules and both of these behaviors were against the rules. Kaleigh came home from practice disappointed in this and told us that unless he quit helping with practice, she was going to quit playing ball. Not only did she tell us this, but Kaleigh also went to her coach and told her what she'd seen and heard and asked if he was going to continue helping with the team. The coach, who was also Kaleigh's math teacher, assured Kaleigh that her brother was just there to help with tryouts and would not be coaching the team. So Kaleigh agreed to play in a pre-season tournament. But when the coach's brother showed up at the tournament, Kaleigh determined there and then that she was quitting softball. When the tournament was over, Kaleigh washed her uniform and packed it in a gallon-size Ziploc bag. On Monday morning as she was putting the bag in her backpack, her dad asked, "What are you doing with your uniform?"

"I'm turning it in. I'm not playing softball anymore," Kaleigh replied.

"Why not?" Dad asked.

"Coach told me her brother wasn't going to be

working with our team, and he was there this weekend. I don't want to play ball anymore. I don't like him chewing tobacco on school grounds and I don't like him cussing when he's with us. I'm quitting."

"Are you sure you want to quit?"

"Yes."

"You don't want to play ball with your sister in high school? I mean, it would be great to get to watch you both play together."

"I'm sorry, Dad. I don't want to play."

"You can't wait a few days and see if you might want to change your mind?"

"No, Dad. I want to quit."

"Are you sure?"

And her dad put Kaleigh through the inquisition for several more minutes. Finally, Kaleigh took her backpack, flung it over her shoulder, kissed her Dad, and said, "I'm sure. I love you, Dad. And I know you want me to play softball. But I don't want to play anymore."

And that was that. I didn't know it then, but that Monday morning, Kaleigh nailed her boundaries. She determined that although she was a part of her father's family, she could also be a part from his desires for her life. She, and only she, could determine her boundaries. This moment in time proved to be pivotal in her life.

3. Take personal responsibility to maintain freedom in love.

I don't know about you, but for me, the hardest

place to maintain good boundaries is in relationships with the people I love the most. And while give-and-take is absolutely necessary in healthy, loving relationships, blurry boundaries are not.

Consider this powerful truth regarding love in relationships. I am quoting Dr. Cloud again: "It is easy to say we love others, but difficult to allow them the freedom inherent in love. When they do not want to do what we want them to, then we 'hunt them down and kill them' in various ways. We pout, cry out angrily, send guilt messages, and attempt to control them. These actions kill freedom and will, and eventually, they will kill love. Love cannot exist without freedom, and freedom cannot exist without responsibility. We must own and take responsibility for what is ours and that includes our disappointment in not getting everything we want from another person. The disappointment that comes from our loved ones exercising their freedom is our responsibility. We must deal with it. This is the only way to keep love alive." [14]

When someone you love lets you down, when their choices or behavior hurt you, you cannot change them, but you can take full responsibility for what you do in response to them. I've known many women who've loved their husbands in spite of their reckless behavior created by infidelity, abuse, and addictions. I've watched these women try desperately to change their husbands. I've heard them make excuses for them and take

---

14 Ibid, pp. 117–118.

ridiculous burdens on themselves to protect their husbands from the natural consequences of their destructive behavior and selfish choices. Many of these women have been nearly crushed under the heavy load they placed on their shoulders. By allowing their husbands' behavior to become their own burdens, these wives have failed to take personal responsibility to maintain freedom in love.

When living this way gets to be too much (and it will), they say things like this to me: "You just don't know what he's done to me!" "He makes me so crazy!" "He's ruining my life." Those are all statements that indicate a breach in boundaries, a broken place in their fences. Their husbands' "stuff" has seeped in and their own "stuff" suffered. The hardest place to maintain healthy boundaries is in relationships with the people we love the most.

The women who come out strong on the other side of these desperate places are the ones who realize that while they cannot do anything to change the behavior of their husbands, they can determine how they will respond. The women who take personal responsibility for their decisions, behavior, and feelings, regardless of the decisions, behavior, and feelings of their husbands, are the women who allow freedom to continue to rule in their marriage. The women who set out to put their husbands together again fail miserably. This is painful indeed, but a much better way to live.

I've used the marriage relationship as an example of

maintaining freedom in love, but this same scenario can take place in any relationship between two people. Are you taking personal responsibility to maintain freedom in love? Do you understand where your limits are in relationship with your loved one? What will it require of you to maintain freedom in this relationship? What do you risk losing? What might you gain? How does your faith factor in to the decisions you are facing?

4. Say what you mean and mean what you say.

When you decide to start establishing healthy boundaries, the people around you will need some time to adjust to the new you. You may need some time to adjust to the new you! And the best way to conquer this season of transition is to say what you mean and mean what you say. Determine to be a person of integrity by sticking to your boundaries. The more you say what you mean and mean what you say, the clearer your boundaries will become to both you and others.

Eventually, the people in your world will respect you more for the confidence you demonstrate by taking full responsibility for your own life and releasing them from meddling in it.

BRINGING THIS BOOK TO A CLOSE

As we've ended with a quick discussion of boundaries, reflect on what you've learned as you've read this book. What are your greatest takeaways? Have you discovered values that resonate with you? If I were to ask you to list three things that are non-negotiables in your life, what would they be?

1. _____

2. _____

3. _____

If I were to ask you how you'd spend your time, if no one else had any expectations of you, how would you spend your time?

I would . . .

What changes are you ready to make?

If you really want to make these changes, make three statements below. Say what you mean and mean what you say:

I want to start . . .

I want to stop . . .

I want to continue . . .

Now, no matter who challenges these things, determine to do them. You get to choose! You get to own your own life. You get to set your limits and you get to live within the limits you set.

You made it! You've done the hard work of getting out of that pity pool. Go get yourself a pack of M&M's and eat every one of them! Keep this book handy, and every once in a while, when you are tempted to start playing the blame game, review the chapters you enjoyed the most. In a few months, go back over the activities you completed at the end of the chapters and do them again.

Be reminded that God is for you and if God is for you, who can be against you? When your back is against the wall and life is coming at you fast, start thanking God for the things you normally take for granted— things like oxygen and legs. Shift your focus from what you feel to what is real and choose to believe.

And most of all, stop blaming others and start taking responsibility for the choices you make.

ABOUT THE AUTHOR

Leighann McCoy is a teacher and motivational speaker. She uses humor joined with deep spiritual insight to encourage others to embrace an intimate personal relationship with God that leads them to partner with Him in His kingdom work. She married Tom McCoy in 1987 and has two daughters, a son, and two grand-daughters; Mikel (Misty and River), Kaleigh, and TJ.

Leighann graduated from Samford University with a Bachelor of Arts degree. She has a Masters of Religious Education degree from Southwestern Baptist Theological Seminary (Ft. Worth, Texas). She and her pastor-husband have been serving in Thompson Station, Tennessee since 1989 where they have seen their congregation grow from eight to over 2,000 in attendance. Today, she splits her time between serving on the Thompson Station Church staff as a prayer and women's minister and participating in her own speaking and writing ministry, Never Fail Faith ministries. But her favorite role is that of "Nana."

Leighann has written several books. Her most recent are: *Spiritual Warfare for Your Family (Bethany House, 2016), Woman's Guide to Hearing God's Voice (2013), Oh God Please! Teach me to Pray,* and *Oh God Please! Help me with my Doubt (2012), and Spiritual Warfare for Women (2011).* She has a new book coming out in early 2017, *Taking Responsibility for the Choices You Make (Dayspring).*